Wise men shun the mistakes of fools.
CATO THE ELDER
c. 200 B.C.

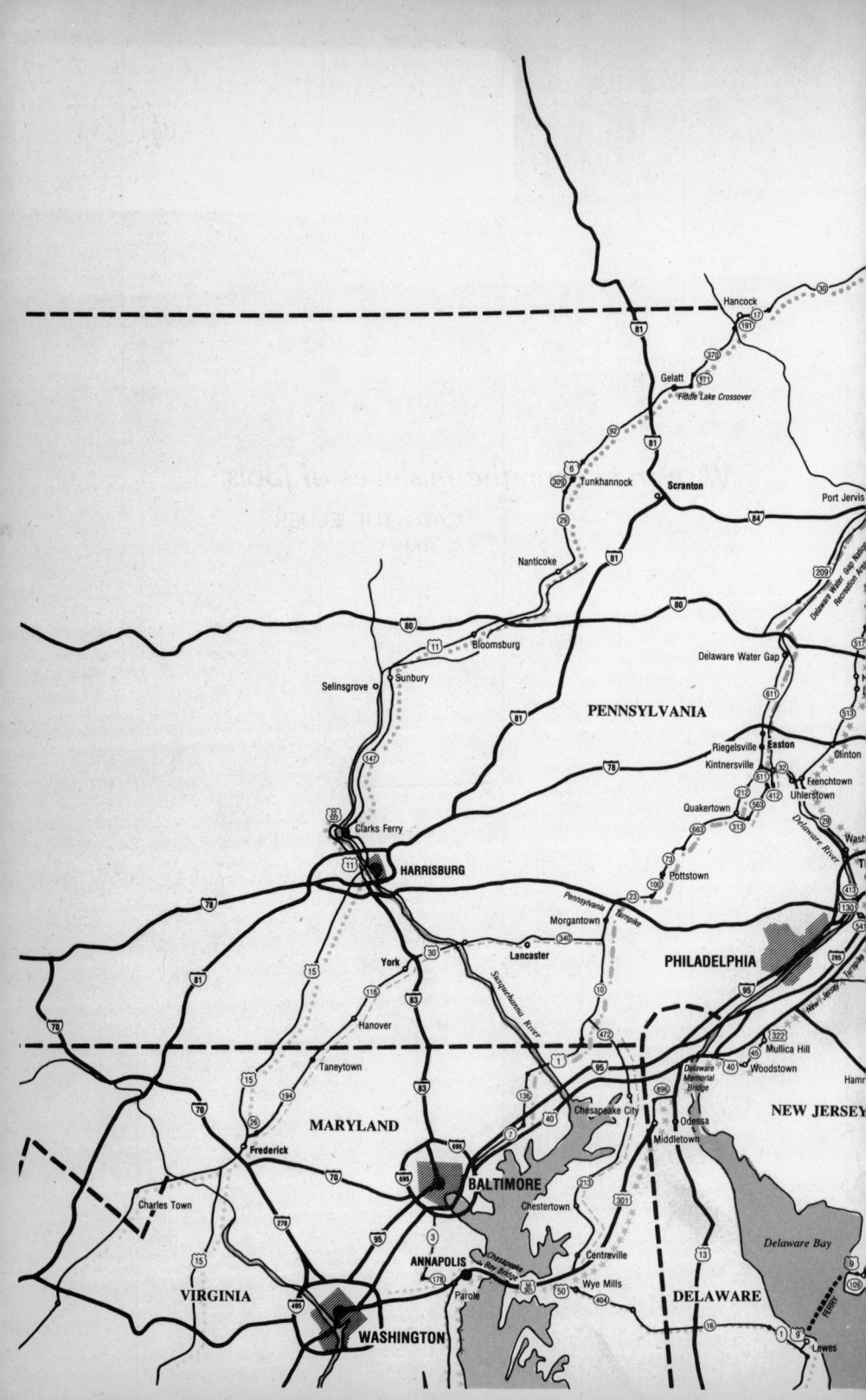

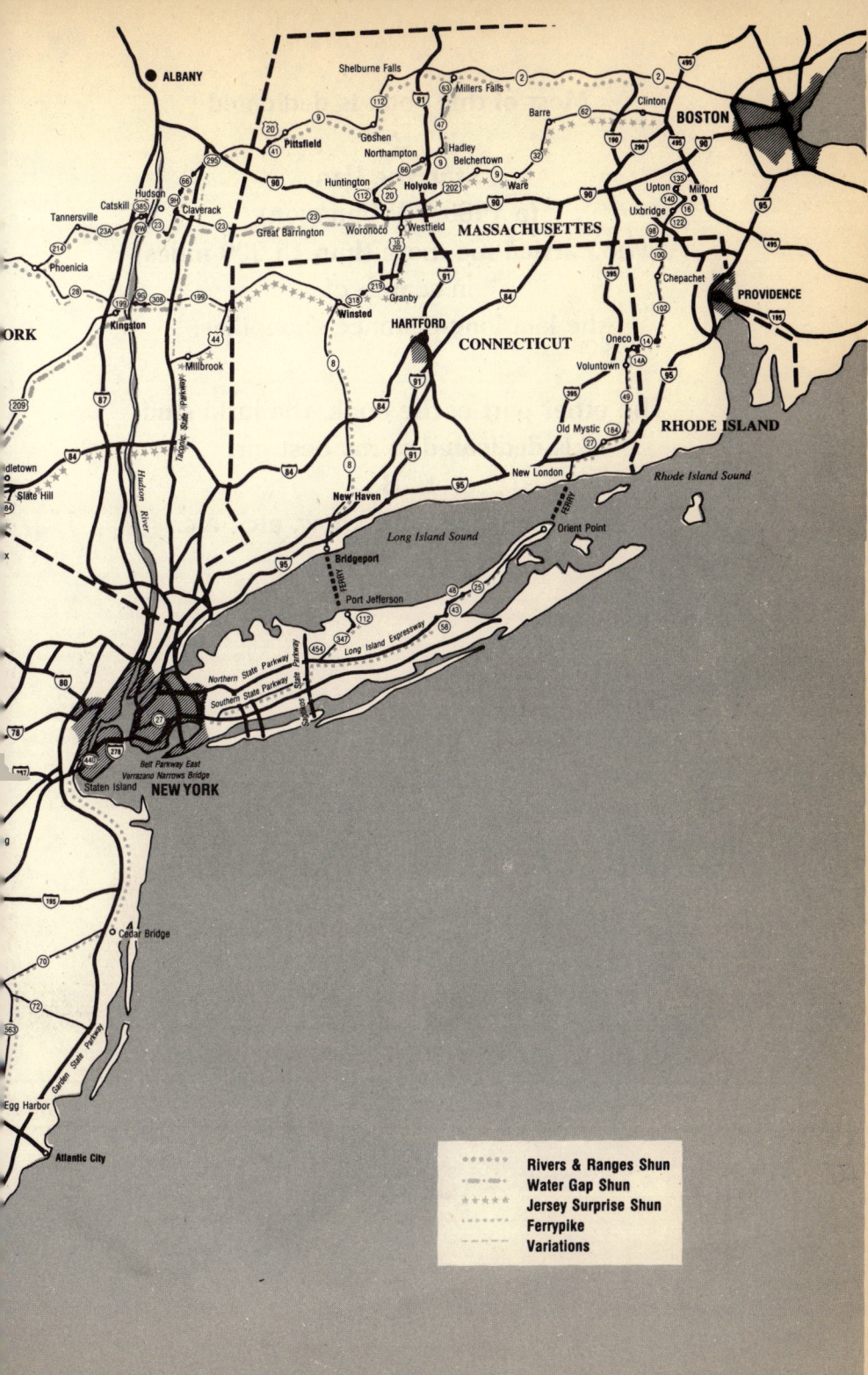

Most of this book is dedicated
to
Stan the Van
(a 1980 VW Vanagon)
who carried me more than 15,000 miles
in search of
the last long-distance shunpikes.

The other part of the book, the lurid stuff,
is dedicated to my best girl
E. B.,
who taught me all I know, etc., etc.

A SHUNPIKER'S GUIDE TO THE NORTHEAST

Washington to Boston
Without Turnpikes or Interstates

Peter Exton

1003 Turkey Run Road   McLean, Virginia 22101

Library of Congress Cataloging-in-Publication Data

Exton, Peter.
  A shunpiker's guide to the Northeast.

  1. Northeastern States—Description and travel—Guidebooks.   I. Title.
  F106.E96   1988   917.4'0443   88-11054
  ISBN 0-939009-10-2

Copyright © 1988 Peter Exton
All Rights Reserved
EPM Publications, Inc., 1003 Turkey Run Road
   McLean, VA 22101
Printed in the United States of America

Cartoons and animation by Melody Sarecky
Cover, maps and book design by Kimberley Roll

Contents

A Personal Note

Of Turnpikers, Shunpikers and Modern American Road Travel

Whither the Highway Hula Doll? 13
The Turnpiker 17
Home of the Turnpiker Faithful: The New Jersey
   Turnpike 19
The Birds 22
Who's Who Out There? 24
The Turnpiker's Motto 25
The Shunpiker's Motto 25

A Shunpiker's Guide to the Northeast

Shunpiking is a State of Mind 28
About Maps 30
Before You Buckle Up—Some Background on the
   Shunpikes 33
Small Town Newspapers 34
Diners 41
X Marks the Spot 44
A Few Words from Our Special Guest 45
Hopping State Lines 46
The Shunpiker's Prayer 48

The Shunpikes:

An Important Note, Especially for Southbound
   Shunpikers 50

The Jersey Surprise Shun 52
   Directions 67
The Rivers and Ranges Shun 81
   Directions 93
The Water Gap Shun 104
   Directions 113

The Ferrypike	120
Directions	129
Variations	142
Epilogue: One Shunpiker's Beginnings	153

List of Maps

Overall map of Shunpikes — ii-iii

Jersey Surprise Shun

Legs 1 and 2	66
Legs 3 and 4	70
Leg 5	76
Leg 6	78

Rivers and Ranges Shun

Leg 1 and Virginia routes bypassing Washington, D.C.	92
Legs 2 and 3	94
Legs 4 and 5	98
Leg 6	102

Water Gap Shun

Legs 1 and 2	112
Leg 3	116
Leg 4	118

Ferrypike

Legs 1, 1-N and 2	128
Legs 3 and 4	132
Legs 5-PJ, 5-OP, 6-B and 6-NL	136

Variations

1 and 2	144
3 and 4	146
5 through 10	150

A Personal Note

My life has been one big shunpike.

In 1970 I went to Seattle, Washington, because a friend swore to me the Pacific Northwest was God's Country. Somewhere in Idaho I met an old woman who asked me where I'd come from.

"Virginia," I said.

"Ahh," she said. "That's God's Country."

A bit later I picked up a hitchhiker in Louisiana who wore a denim jacket with "Apostles" stitched on the back. This man testified that God's Country is situated between two remote bayous loaded with catfish. Of course the exact location could not be told, owing to the fact that an apostle is also a fisherman and a good fisherman would never divulge the whereabouts of a dandy fishing hole, especially if God owns the property.

In 1975 I was driving with friends on Massachusetts Route 2 from a place called Still River into Boston when I asked to be taken to Logan Airport. I landed in Denver, Colorado, with $10 in my pocket, and promptly bought two records: a collection of Irish folk songs and *The Best Of Woody Guthrie*. I did not have a record player.

In 1981 some of the greatest names in popular music made it clear to me that Nashville was not ready for my songs. I went home to Arlington, Virginia. I needed lodging. The Sunday classifieds said two rooms were available in a group house. Rushing over at about noon I was told that a determined woman from New Hampshire had already claimed the $90 room. I settled for the $120 room in the basement. By 1983 I had wed the gal from the Granite State and we were making trips to New Hampshire several times each year. She called them visits to God's Country. On one of these trips we got stuck in one too many turnpike-turned-parking lot traffic jams. At the earliest opportunity we escaped, never to return.

And thus and thus and so and so it was that I set out to write this book.

Of Turnpikers, Shunpikers and Modern American Road Travel

Dese are de conditions dat prevail.
JIMMY DURANTE

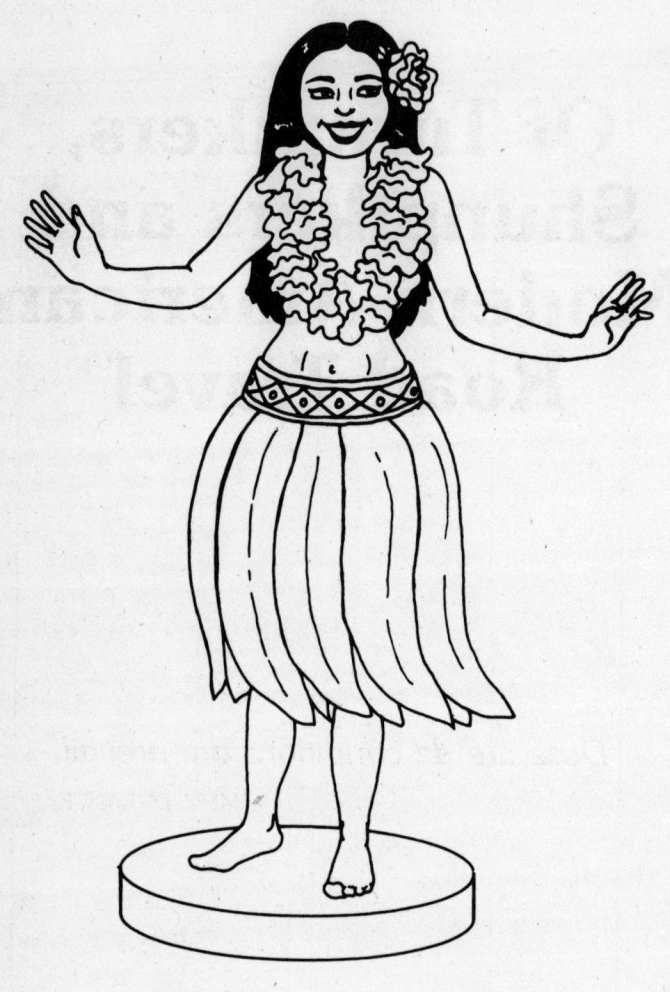

Whither the Highway Hula Doll?

Modern man thinks with his bulldozer.

JOHN ORMSBEE SIMONDS
Landscape Architect

Whatever happened to the highway Hula Doll? Maybe you can remember: She once stood proudly in the rear window of America's automobiles wearing only a flower lei and a grass skirt. She was just plastic, of course, with plastic hair and plastic flowers molded to her chest, but she was carefree and happy, just like the folks who had put her there on the shelf behind the back seat, next to the box of Kleenex. Part of the fun was giving the rubber suction cup on her base a good lick so she'd stay firmly in place.

She didn't just stand there, though. My, oh my, no. Under that skirt her thigh bone was connected to her waist bone by a lively, coiled spring, and with every dip and turn in the road she bopped around like nobody's business. The deeper the dip, the sharper the turn, the better she danced. She caught her breath on the straightaways.

Hula Doll went everywhere. She went to the Wash-O-Mat and G.C. Murphy and the A&W Root Beer stand. She dropped the family off at Griffith Stadium where the Senators played ball, back when first place meant a pennant and last place had no company, except in the National League. Every summer she took grandma to either Cape May or Provincetown, and she once went to Newport to listen to a guy named Herbie Mann.

She went to the mountains and stayed at motels that weren't part of a chain of look-alike lodgings. The mountain roads were ideal for dancing; they snaked along ancient streambeds and sometimes through steep gorges and out to the edge of a cliff. The kids shrieked and said it was scary, but they giggled when they said it.

Hula Doll went to the beach, though she never went in the water. She was content to wait for the gang to return and tell Aunt Hula all about crabs and nettles and stuff. She understood that we all have our lot in life. Sometimes they brought her pretty pieces of broken pop bottles, rounded down nicely by surf and sand.

When the oldest boy went to college Hula Doll learned some fun things they don't teach on family trips. Like S.O.B. turns: The young undergrad would politely open the door and seat his date on the passenger side of the plastic-covered bench seat, then put himself behind the wheel. Cruising along down Main, steering with the heel of his left hand, he would accelerate slightly, then hit the brake and whip the car hard right down a side street. He'd raise his right arm, murmur "Slide over baby" (S.O.B.), and catch the helpless co-ed as momentum carried her across the length of the seat. Hula Doll went wild.

Later on she learned to go parking. She would wait for the windows to fog up and then dance quietly in the dark when the young romantics made undulatin' motions to the hepcat rhythms on the radio.

Hula Doll was tough, too. She could spend all afternoon under a blistering sun and never lose a curl or get a burn. Once in a while the kids would bat her around just for fun until she touched her ear to an ankle, and then with a frozen little hand-painted smile she'd stand right up and say do it again, that's why I'm here.

But mostly Hula Doll liked dancing down the road, rolling with the landscape, counting the cows and watching the Mail Pouch barns go by.

Then came turnpikes and interstates.

Maybe the people who built these roads just couldn't dance, and so took aim at Hula Doll's pleasure. Maybe they all cheated on the same roadbuilder's test and were graduated without knowing squat about curling a gentle S-curve

through the woods. Or maybe their only tool was a level.

Whatever the reason, these people built what they called super highways, the turnpikes and interstates. For them, the only good landscape was a dead landscape.

Even the gentlest rise in the swelling breast of God's Country succumbed to the bulldozer's blade. Purple mountains' majesty buckled and fell, trucked off as landfill in the annoying dells and dales. The sweet chirping of birdies and the donk of the moo-cow's bell were replaced by the angry howl of high-speed engines screaming toward the sound barrier.

Hula Doll was overwhelmed. These weren't roads; they were trajectories. Surveyors set up their tripods in Washington and peered straight through to Boston along highways as flat as a tollgate operator's smile.

Flat highways; straight highways. The auto makers' firing range. Boxes of motionless people hurtling through space. A kind of low altitude earth orbit.

Before long, it was clear the turnpike builders had also fashioned a new horizon: two guardrails and the slow end of a truck. Behind? The fast end of another truck, without brakes, crawling into your back seat.

Bordered by rails and fences topped with barbed wire, the turnpikes and interstates resembled long cattle chutes, the livestock herded along within. There was an occasional gate or ramp where the beef could be off-loaded and then gobbled up by the cities, but feed bins and watering troughs were installed right on the roadway to discourage potential strays from wandering off to greener pastures.

The innocent public was unaware they'd become a part of a massive cattle drive. By the 1970s just about every long-distance road traveler on the continent had been corralled onto the turnpikes and interstates.

The era of the open range in American travel had come to an end, and the art of travel had been completely reshaped.

Gone were the ups and downs and S-curves that had moved Hula Doll to shake her happy hips. The bop and roll of the ribbon highway had become the endless drone of cruise control. Children who once shouted "wheee!"

when their tiny tummies felt a dip in the road began to grumble and whine, their promising minds beaten numb by never-changing scenery and the bullet line of a zero percent grade. They were left only to count down mileposts to the end of their torment.

Hula Doll danced no more.

The word went out across the land. "Hula Doll's A Stiff!," the headlines read. For a while thoughtful columnists tried to analyze her sudden change, and popularized the myth that Hula Doll's way of dancing had simply gone out of style. They never thought about looking at the roads. Before long most people couldn't remember that Hula Doll had ever danced at all.

Her spunk was gone. She lost her tone. Her spring got rusty.

Tears down their cheeks, children begged Hula Doll to dance. She just stood there, solemn and cruel, staring bleakly out the rear window at the Mack Truck bulldog snarling in her face. The kids smacked her up-side her plastic hibiscus, but she was no more lively than a church full of white people trying to sing hymns. (Occasionally, when a huge tractor-trailer blasted by, she wiggled a little.)

By the time the youngest boy went to college all the dorms had gone co-ed, ending young love's need for S.O.B. turns and behind-the-stadium parking. Comfy American bench seats were replaced by foreign buckets, and Hula Doll was left out in the cold.

It was no use. Hula Doll never went anywhere but straight ahead, and that was no cause for dancing. The young kids, the innocent ones, blamed her for their misery. How could they know otherwise? They ripped her off the shelf and tossed her out the window. She smashed into brutal concrete and shattered into itsy bitsy pieces.

She was nothing but litter now, and nobody paid her fine.

The Turnpiker

When we get these thruways across the whole country...it will be possible to drive from New York to California without seeing a single thing.

JOHN STEINBECK
Travels With Charley

Over the fractured fragments of Hula Doll's once bop-lively torso rolled a new kind of traveler: the turnpiker.

The turnpiker was willing to give up all his travel freedom for the promise of speed. He exchanged the open road for a controlled environment surrounded by barriers, fences and guard rails. His movements were analyzed and dissected, like a lab rat in a very long maze. He got on these highways where he was told, gassed up and rested where he was told, ate what and where he was told. In the end he also got off the highway where he was told, sometimes even paying for the privilege.

There was no scenery, save for looking at other rats in the maze.

With speed as their god the turnpikers fisted their hands around steering wheels and charged forward like punch-drunk boxers on the attack. "Let's barrel!" they sometimes howled. Brows and shoulders tensed, they raced along the new concrete deserts pursuing an endless dotted line, like dogs chasing their tails.

(Turnpikes promised speed, but the promise was regularly broken with sinister traffic jams in the name of "Construction Ahead—Expect Delays." The propoganda went out that construction would bring yet more speed, but the turnpike builders simply moved the signs around, teasing the helplessly addicted turnpikers.)

The art of travel had reached an all-time low. The turnpikers had but one goal—to be someplace else. Whatever lay between was an obstacle to be overcome. "The hell with travel," they said.

And thus and thus and so and so it was that the first turnpikers came to be. And they begat more turnpikers. This begetting begat more begetting, and lo, the nation was soon dominated by this obedient, submissive herd.

Over the years, the turnpikers have developed a way of traveling that is something like sleepwalking: The eyes are open but nothing is seen, and upon waking the turnpiker is someplace other than where he started. What happens in between is neither experienced nor remembered.

The car acts as a time-cocoon; sealed inside, the turnpiker activates climate, sound and speed controls, and then coats his eyes with a blank gaze. Emerging from the cocoon some hours later, he knows only that the setting has changed and he must use a different set of keys to enter a building. For all he knows, it was the earth did the moving while he remained in place.

Time passed, and when enough turnpikers had been reared on the turnpikes and interstates, no one any longer thought to question that travel could be any different. And so it is: Along the super highways there aren't any side roads, so nobody looks to turn down one. At the one-choice-only restaurants nobody asks for a hamburger medium-rare, because everybody knows you can't get it. Nobody pulls over and stops on impulse because you're dead if you try, and nobody hopes to see any beautiful views because nobody expects one.

Limited access means no escape.

Home of the Turnpiker Faithful: The New Jersey Turnpike

O! that way madness lies; let me shun that.

KING LEAR

Like Mecca, Santa's lap, Fenway Park and Elvis's Graceland, the New Jersey Turnpike is the ultimate hangout for true believers, in this case the turnpiker faithful. Built by and for turnpikers, owned and operated by turnpikers, it has everything a turnpiker could hope for: no scenery, no turns, no choices, no hope and plenty of company.

From their headquarters in a bleak 1950s building overlooking the Turnpike in New Brunswick, the Turnpiker Lords survey the madness they have wrought. And each year about 200 million cars, buses and trucks (including 100,000 serpents with six or more axles) roll by under their satisfied noses.

The four billion miles traveled by these vee-hickles (police talk) generate about $2 million in annual business for toll ticket makers. Each toll ticket is dispersed by a machine that sticks its tongue out at you so you can grab it. Then the tickets and tolls are collected by tollgate operators, none of whom has heard that it takes 56 muscles to frown and only 17 to smile.

As of this writing, 4.53 million toll tickets remain lost in dashboard nooks and heater vents.

On a slow day in January you and 250,000 others congregate on the turnpike. Make that a hot million around summer holidays. And every year police hand out 75,000 tickets and 20,000 warnings on the Turnpike.

Thirteen eating establishments along the Turnpike offer travelers no choice: Roy Rogers or Bob's Big Boy. (All right, one choice, but haven't you noticed that chain food is all the same?—only the packaging changes. Wouldn't you love to know how much you're paying for food and how much for packaging? Maybe not. Would it leave a bitter taste in your mouth to find out you're paying more for styrofoam than for your roadmeat burger?) And by the way, you no longer eat *meals*, at least not in the fast food joints. Industry insiders have added up your typical day and spat it out in tasty jargon: The moment you spend swallowing their food is called an "eating episode." Bon appetit, and pass the secret sauce, whatever it's made of.

New Jersey's Turnpiker Lords have hosted visitors from places like France, Italy, China, Japan, Korea, Israel, Brazil and even South Africa. It is not known if they have hosted anyone from New Jersey. It is not known why anyone wants to come. It is also unclear where the hosts took their visitors to dinner, Roy Rogers or Bob's Big Boy. And if they went to the Big Boy, did the guests stay or did they go?

The New Jersey Turnpike, which has a population that certainly warrants one, just might be the only road in the world with its own newspaper, *The Trailblazer*. Somebody once wrote the paper's editor suggesting the service area names be changed to honor people who had logged the most miles on the turnpike and paid the most money in tolls. He suggested biographies be published of "these important people who call the turnpike home." The Turnpiker Lords declined to take this unique opportunity to recognize a deserving few, but they did honor a thousand turnpikers with NJTP charge accounts, billed weekly.

According to a recent annual report of the New Jersey Turnpike Authority (the official name of the Turnpiker Lords), somebody in charge there wanted to plant some trees. For this it was necessary to institute a program. The program then had to have a name: Turnpike Region Environmental Enrichment program, or TREE. The prospect of having trees along the Turnpike generated a lot of excitement within the turnpiker community, so a ceremony was held to give the saplings a proper welcome. The governor showed up to receive a wooden plaque. A band played, speeches were made, photos were taken. No trees had survived earlier programs, so the ceremony took place under a tent.

A year later, under the heading "Maintenance," the annual report mentioned that the Landscape Section was seen "actively renovating flower beds." The idea of renovation taking place in a flower bed was a new one to me. Active renovation, no less. Those tiny little seeds and seedlings must have been overwhelmed with all the busy, busy activity. Let's hope they got a little water. Meanwhile, "an evaluation of Plant Growth Regulators was initiated." The objective was to "reduce grass growth" by pouring chemicals on the ground, thereby trimming the need for mowing and "manpower utilization." This last phrase has something to do with the guys who push the mowers, I think, and is the type of turnpiker language that turns one-line statements into 50-page reports.

So on the one hand, the Turnpiker Lords say they want to enrich the environment by planting trees along the Turnpike. Yet on the other hand, they are hoping to stunt plant growth by treating grass with things not found in nature. What gives? Do they want plants to grow or don't they? In light of their desire to make rye and fescue bow down to their will, where do these people find the gall to name a rest area for Walt Whitman, author of *Leaves of Grass*?

> *Give me the splendid silent sun with all his*
> *   beams full-dazzling,*
> *Give me juicy autumnal fruit ripe and red from*
> *   the orchard,*
> *Give me a field where the unmow'd grass*
> *   grows,*
> *Give me an arbor, give me the trellis'd grape,*
> *Give me fresh corn and wheat, give me serene-*
> *   moving animals teaching content,*
> *Give me nights perfectly quiet...*
>
>   WALT WHITMAN
>   *Leaves Of Grass*

The Birds

There is a rumor that Alfred Hitchcock drew the inspiration for his classic horror film *The Birds* from traveling on an interstate. He was terrified by the birds he saw there. They were all black or dark gray and lurked on posts staring at traffic. Some of them were carrion eaters. Most of them had greasy-looking feathers, as if they'd bathed in service area oil slicks. There wasn't a bluebird, goldfinch or bright red cardinal anywhere. Just vultures, crows, starlings, pigeons, grackles. And ravens. Shades of asphalt. Hitchcock later had a bad dream, the rumor goes, about a world swarming with such turnpiker birds, and it scared him enough to do a movie that would give everybody the creeps.

Next time you're traveling an interstate, check out the birds. They all look tarred and feathered. Imagine! Going from Washington to Boston along interstates it's possible to see only tar-colored birds. Five hundred miles of tar birds. That's really creepy. Tar birds, tar road, tar burgers. These highways are completely void of color, a black-and-white world within a full-color universe. November every day of the year. Don't even go if it's overcast.

Why don't we see any yellow birds along the interstates? Or red ones, or blue ones? Where do they go?

You'll find them in forests, along rivers and in small towns. They hang out with flowers and trees and green fields. They go where shunpikers go.

Who's Who Out There?

Before we make like bluebirds and go where the shunpikers go, let's be clear about who's who out there:

A **turnpiker**
   a) can look at a map of a thousand roads and see only an interstate;
   b) is a human lemming who travels in herds, synchronizes his bladder with rest areas, is usually harried and tense, and hates what he's doing while meekly accepting it as unavoidable;
   c) follows the beaten rut.

A **shunpiker**
   a) can look at one road and ask: Why not another?;
   b) is an independent traveler who has found peace and tranquility, maybe romance and a better job, but surely a great roadside diner, by breaking away from turnpikes and the interstate highway system;
   c) goes his own way.

The Turnpiker's Motto

Rut is right.

The Shunpiker's Motto

The victor is he who can go it alone.

A Shunpiker's Guide to the Northeast

*Over the river and through the woods
To grandmother's house we go!*

　　　　　　FROM AN OLD SHUNPIKER
　　　　　　SPIRITUAL

Shunpiking is a State of Mind

There's absolutely no reason for being rushed along with the rush. Everybody should be free to go very slow...What you want, what you're hanging around in the world waiting for, is for something to occur to you.

ROBERT FROST

More than anything else, shunpiking is a state of mind. It is like ballooning in the jet age. The jet covers a distance quickly, but the traveler sees virtually nothing of that distance. The balloonist, on the other hand, purposely makes time to see, feel and smell everything around him. And like ballooning, shunpiking isn't something you have to do; it is a voluntary time out from routine, from rushing along with the rush. And it's a way to invite that something to occur to you, in a place not buried by asphalt and concrete.

You don't have to go where the mapmakers have drawn the thick lines—go where you choose to go.

Shunpiking is possibilities, suggestions, the persuasion of a four-year-old. You have a destination, but you're not out to break any speed records getting there. You're looking for the antithesis of rush hour: a road that is fun to drive and takes you away from your daily experiences.

To get your mind going in the right direction, you must mentally shift into an unhurried gear and *relax*. Everything else in successful shunpiking flows from that. Repeat the word *relax* again and again until you understand it, especially if you feel yourself falling into turnpiker anxiousness.

(To ward off a surge of turnpiker tension, make a periodic check of your shoulder muscles. Keep them relaxed.)

If it will help put you at ease, pretend shunpiking is an ancient oriental exercise (it is true that relaxation is the single most important concept in practicing the centuries-old Chinese exercise t'ai-chi). Make each curve to the left a *yin* and each curve to the right a *yang*. Together they balance the road, and thereby the universe, and thus you are traveling the way of peace, nirvana and transcendental whoop-deedo. Why not? People get serious about more cockeyed notions. Just think of all those turnpikers who act as if driving is a martial art.

Unnecessary haste can conspire to ruin a relaxed shunpiking state of mind, not to mention the balance of the universe. There are a few things that can be done to eliminate haste and better your chances of enjoying the trip:

●Don't promise to be there for dinner. Deadlines are necessary evils of the workaday world*, but there is no reason to inflict such pressures on yourself when traveling. By its nature shunpiking is an open-ended style of travel; restricting your fun just to eat meatloaf at six doesn't make good sense.

●Leave earlier than you need to. There are few things so invigorating as being on the road ahead of schedule. If 7:30 A.M. is when you should leave, get off an hour earlier. Crossing a state line at 7:00 A.M. will make you feel terrific. And knowing you're on top of things, with time to stop if something occurs, will enhance the relaxation part.

●Bring unsweetened apple juice for refreshment, instead of soda pop. I am convinced that haste is a nasty, and potentially dangerous, side-effect of drinking soda pop, which is full of sugar and caffeine. Those ingredients make people antsy, and antsy people can't relax. They speed. Pouring sugar and caffeine into people confined in a small space for several hours is like pouring kerosene into a pot sitting on a warm stove burner. Give it time and it will explode. Those who dodge sugar-coated teeth by drinking diet soda are fooling themselves. Sugar substitutes roll

---

*Editor's note: Author did not make deadline on this delightfully relaxed book.

around in stomachs and re-emerge in the form of bad breath. Caffeine and a carload of bad breath may contribute more to haste than regular soda. Who wants to prolong an exposure to foul air?

I am fond of the little six-packs of apple juice in cans. Tuck those babies under the ice in your cooler for a while; when thirst strikes, they are unbeatable quenchers.

About Maps

In searching for shunpikes, I have used road maps provided by the state tourism offices as my main references. With very few exceptions, they show everything necessary for finding your way and include lots of other detail. They tell you neat things about each state, like its nickname and motto, official state animals and plants, points of interest and recreational facilities. New Jersey goes so far as to include the state insect (honeybee) and a handy list of penalties for various driving offenses. There is almost always an enthusiastic "Dear Traveler" message from the current or recently defeated governor, accompanied by a portrait suitable for altering with a pencil.

Although I give directions here for each shunpike and have included maps indicating their routes, I strongly recommend building a collection of state road maps, which are free for the asking. There's no hassle involved, each map being only a phone call away. Some of the calls are tolled, but it won't take more than 30 seconds to say, "I'd like a road map of your state. My address is. . ." You might also add that you are leaving in two weeks, and ask if it would be possible to send the map right away first class. Some states, Massachusetts especially, have the damnedest troubles addressing an envelope, slipping a map in it, and licking the stamp.

Here are the numbers to call:

State	Phone
Connecticut	(800) 243-1685
Delaware	(800) 441-8846
Maine	(207) 289-2423
Maryland	(800) 331-1750
Massachusetts	(617) 727-3201
New Hampshire	(603) 271-2666
New Jersey	(609) 292-2470
New York	(518) 474-4116
Rhode Island	(401) 277-2601
Pennsylvania	(800) VISIT-PA
Vermont	(802) 828-3236
Virginia	(800) VISIT-VA
West Virginia	(800) CALL-WVA

I am not against the large atlases put out annually by AAA, Gousha, Rand McNally and others, but these books are designed for turnpikers. Turnpikes and interstates are well drawn, and much attention seems to be given to keeping that kind of information up to date. But other roads, good ones, are included only when space allows. Many,

many roads simply aren't drawn; many that are don't have route numbers. (A lot of help that is.) These atlases can be useless if you are trying to circle around a monster traffic jam; at best they require lots of guesswork.

Some information given in these atlases is outdated or just plain wrong. Particularly irritating is the practice, if not the idea, of designating scenic routes. Why don't Rand McNally and AAA agree on what's a scenic route through Pennsylvania Dutch country? I have the strong impression that AAA marked PA23 east of Lancaster as scenic about 25 or 30 years ago but hasn't been back since. The present scenery is essentially a shopping strip. Meanwhile, Rand McNally takes us on a scenic route (US222) from Lancaster north to Reading, or more accurately, through Reading. I turned back after several miles of stoplights and suburban shopping centers. It's enough to make me suspicious when I see that Rand McNally has marked the entire length of the Pennsylvania Turnpike a scenic route. That includes Breezewood, the self-proclaimed Town of Motels.

While I'm griping, I may as well vent my big beef about these atlases: They carry so much advertising they're beginning to look like a commercial strip on old US1. Rand McNally is the main culprit. The maps are wrapped in page after page of ads and coupons for motels (I suppose we should be thankful there's no such thing as blinking neon ink) and amusements like safari world animal kingdom theme park museums. If you want to use the U.S. mileage map, you've got to wade through ads to find it. I buy magazines for ads; I buy reference books for reference. An atlas is for reference. Rand might protest that advertising helps keep down the cost of the atlas. Maybe. But I see the expense of producing all those extra color pages that don't have to be there.

AAA isn't quite so bad. They only promote AAA products, and there are fewer ads. But in the first paragraph of the introduction called About the Atlas, they tell us to keep their book in mind as a gift for birthdays and Christmas. Seems the ads have dribbled over into the book text. Maybe next year the atlas will have a section called How to Use This Book that will tell us how to Buy Ten--Get One Free.

Before You Buckle Up—
Some Background on the Shunpikes

Now that your mind is in the right place and you've got all the state road maps you need, let me tell you a little bit about what lies ahead.

I have been criss-crossing the northeastern United States regularly for more than two decades. I like the looks of this land and have been saddened by the increasing temptation people have of characterizing an entire state by the few things they are able to glimpse from the interstates and turnpikes. Such people are turnpikers and know nothing, believe me. In the last 18 months I set out to explore all sorts of roads that were free of congestion and full of things to see along the way. I was determined not to feel chained to the interstate highway system, and at the same time I was convinced I could find combinations of enjoyable routes that would take me comfortably from Washington to Boston. Much to my satisfaction and relief, and I hope to yours, I was able to put together four major shunpikes running from near Washington to Boston's I-495 and ten variations that can help keep things new for many trips to come.

Each of the shunpikes has been named for a significant feature of the route, which I think is more fun than just numbering them. Thus we have: the *Jersey Surprise Shun*, which drives home my point about mistaken impressions taken by turnpikers; the *Rivers and Ranges Shun*, because you'll see plenty of both streams and mountains; the *Water Gap Shun*, which at its midpoint runs through the Delaware Water Gap National Recreation Area; and the *Ferrypike*, a seafaring solution to rounding New York City to the east. The variations are routes that connect the above shunpikes to each other, so you can travel parts of two or more.

Roads and scenery aren't the only things that make shunpiking worth the ride. In the following pages I discuss the joys of reading somebody else's local newspaper—even the classifieds are fun for comparison shopping—and of sitting down for a meal at one of the last of the diners that used to feed all travelers. The small section X Marks the Spot should be read by anyone of consenting age.

By now you've probably gathered that seriousness is not one of my vices. It comes and goes, but most of the time I like to be gay, as my grandmother used to say, as in "We had such a gay time on the carousel." Another fellow who always enjoys an old-fashioned gay time is the irrepressible Mr. Toad, who has been around as long as the century. (I met him in my youth when my father would read me a chapter of *The Wind in the Willows* at bedtime.) After some tricky negotiations, Toad has agreed to make a brief appearance to help illustrate the Toad Memorial Hop. (It was the flattery of naming the Hop in his honor that finally won him over.)

Small Town Newspapers

How could anybody not buy a copy of the *Daily Item*, the hometown paper of Clinton, Massachusetts? Only 25 cents and you get 12 pages—"plus supplements"—under a name that sounds like teen romance. In between *Daily* and *Item* at the top of the front page is a line drawing of a pumphouse and the dam that looms above this old mill town. No splayed eagles clutching ribbons and arrows, no Greek figures robed in heroic Latin phrases. Just the wall that holds back the water and the stump of a building that measures it out. And why not? They are the steady heartbeat of dear old Clinton.

The *Daily Item* news stories are almost entirely local. Sprinkled among them are birth, retirement and auction announcements, tributes, poems, a thought for the day, the Elks Lodge bingo date and an advertisement for bark mulch. There's also a curious "chain" prayer to God (read Santa Claus). "The person must say this prayer for three consecutive days. After three days the favor requested will be granted." When your wish comes true you've got to put the prayer (and the instructions) in the paper, but don't tell anybody what you wished for and leave only your initials at the bottom.

Even though Clinton is just a long fly ball from Boston,

the Red Sox and Celtics play second fiddle to sports stories like "Nashoba pounds Murdock," "Clinton tops Algonquin," and "Tahanto wins 2nd game." The local kids are what matter most here. Roger Clemens and Larry Bird can pursue world championships in big city papers; in the *Item* it's girls' softball: Jodi Sylvester's clutch pinch hit to keep the ninth-inning rally alive and Amy Moriarty's heartbreak at having walked in the winning run.

On the entertainment page:

For all you know, that leggy babe in stiletto heels, garters and body suit who plays a Hot Box Dancer in the Clinton Community Theater's rendition of *Guys and Dolls* is the mother of five. She might also be the town librarian, whose lights always go out before ten and who drives a mud brown Plymouth. Or she's the bank vice-president; a novelist; a church deacon; a chemist. Maybe even a pipe smoker. Best of all, she might be the Chief of Pumphouse Operations. Small towns like Clinton afford lots of opportunity to try one's wings, and papers like the *Item* are always there to record them.

Rounding out the last few of the daily 12 pages are stories like "Trial faces its second mistrial" and "Clinton man found not guilty in bumper attack" (the bumper was not attached to a car), and comics, horoscopes, a crossword puzzle, grocery ads and the classifieds. Between "Services" and "Apartments" in the classifieds are ten ads under the mysterious heading "Lucky 7." Meaning? I think these ads—for a variety of things from windows and stainless steel cooktops to an organ—run seven days for the price of one, or something like that.

The *Daily Item*, which has been around since 1893, isn't printed in anything but black ink, and its paper yellows soon enough. It isn't noted for its coverage of world, or even state, affairs. What it has to say isn't of much importance to folks who've never lived beneath the great dam. It's just another little paper that serves its community, from the mayor to the chain-prayer faithful. It's wonderful.

I'm not sure why I love reading the *Daily Item*s of America when I'm shunpiking. I live in the suburbs of a big city and my daily newspaper doesn't care at all what goes on in my neighborhood. I'm fascinated by the fact that the Clinton High School woodworking class warrants a picture and story on Page One. I have been lonely in my big city; the *Daily Item* makes Clinton seem so warm and friendly. If I hit a home run here, or drop a pop fly, everybody in town will know it. If for no other reason, I guess I like reading small town papers to find out what my countrymen and women are doing with their lives.

It takes only a few issues of small town newspapers to find out who's the most popular person in America. It's certainly no politician. It's no movie or sports star either.

It's the fireman. He's got a dangerous, exciting job and he saves puppies and teddy bears. When he puts on his work clothes and rushes off to a fire, everybody knows he's there to protect. For this he is honored with more appearances on the front page of small town papers than anybody else, and not a journalist anywhere would say a bad thing about him. He's pictured in his fire engine, in his uniform and famous chapeau. He is frequently shown at the local elementary school teaching youngsters the evils of leaving rags in closets, and sometimes he takes the whole class for a ride on Big Red No. 3, the vintage town fire engine. The lucky kids get to put on his hat.

There are four other consistently popular subjects worthy of large photo and story space on the front page of local papers:

Coming in a distant second to the firemen are policemen. We sometimes get to see them training with guns. They teach the kids hand signals for safe bike riding and how to fingerprint each other. They too have neato uniforms, with shiny things.

Next are local school activities, which range from the solemn induction of students into an honor society to teen lovelies spinning parasols as part of rehearsal for the school beauty pageant. Parents who volunteer to help out with school activities stand a pretty good chance of getting their picture in the paper, especially if they are mothers.

Then comes the oddball stuff. Like the old man who still insists on getting back and forth to town on his mule. Or the guy who's teaching his pet crow to talk because somebody said it couldn't be done. A few of these stories arise out of disaster, such as the cows standing on the farmer's roof after the flood waters have receded. Oddball is a popular subject inside these papers as well, and just might be the overall number one favorite.

Number five in the most popular subject category is "heritage" festivals. Curiously, most American towns were founded on a sunny weekend in May or June. I know this because that's when the Founder's Day festivals take place. It makes sense to me. Would you go running around in the wilderness looking to start a ville in snowbound January or the heat and buggy humidity of August?

Obviously, the festivals would rank a little higher than they do if they were spread throughout the year. And they deserve more attention simply because they bring out the firemen, policemen, school groups and oddballs.

On page three of the 20-page *Carroll County Times* (Maryland) was a picture of a man holding a block of something in one hand and a small figure in the other. The caption, in tall boldface, said "Sanding." One line explained that Doug Moeller, age 28, was sanding a clay elephant outside his home on Klee Mill Road. That was it. Nothing more.

This may seem a waste of space to those accustomed to big city newspapers. Not so. Local papers don't confine themselves exclusively to news, and nobody wants them to. They provide a service. In this instance it is the single women of the area who are well served. Not only do they know where to go for all their clay elephants, they can see that this guy isn't wearing a wedding ring. He's handsome too, and his hair is full and dark and his arms and shoulders are straining admirably in his shirt. He's obviously handy. His fingernails are clean and he can sand his elephant while wearing sunglasses. He lives on Klee Mill Road, in case you want to drive by and shop elephants.

A photo of Doug and his sanding is no waste at all. And it's a lot safer than turning the space over to the advice columnist.

The Hunterdon County Democrat. It's been around since 1825, a lot longer than *The New York Times, Washington Post* or *Boston Globe.* Under its name is this declaration: "An Independent Newspaper, Dedicated to the Principles of True Democracy—Not a Party Organ." In bold print a "Net Press Run" of 27,500 is announced. Published weekly at Flemington, New Jersey. Cost: 50 cents.

Here are some other long-time practitioners of freedom of the press, along with things they like to say about themselves:

The Fauquier Democrat (Virginia): Fauquier's Family Newspaper Since 1817.

Kent County News (Maryland): A Direct Descendant Of *The Chestertown Spy,* Est. 1793.

The Express (New Jersey): Serving Pennsylvania and New Jersey Since 1855.

Ocean County Observer (New Jersey): "The only daily newspaper committed exclusively to Ocean County." Since 1850.

The Globe-Times (Pennsylvania): The Voice Of Bethlehem Since 1867 (has a nice biblical ring to it, don't you think?).

In York, Pennsylvania, two evidently well established papers seem to be carrying on a very old competition for readership: The *York Daily Record* calls itself "York's first newspaper" and says how many years it's been around, 173 in 1988. *The York Dispatch* claims to be "Today's News Today," as afternoon papers often do, and says a bunch of other stuff too: Home Delivered Edition (I bought mine at a newsstand); Circulation Books Always Open; Copy 25

Cents PAY NO MORE. My copy also said "Vol. 222, NO. 36" on July 10, 1986. If volume number means year of operation, the *Dispatch* goes back to 1764. Except that would make it older than the *Daily Record*, which claims to be York's first paper. The *Dispatch* looks really old. Eight narrow columns fill the front page, and there are no photos. The *Daily Record* tries to appear more contemporary, using diagrams and colors à la *USA Today*. Inside on the masthead the *Record* states plainly that it was founded in 1815. The *Dispatch* says it was founded by Hiram Young, no date. Absolutely everyone on the money end of the *Dispatch* is a Young, even the Assistant Secretary-Treasurer. My guess is that the *York Daily Record* is actually the older paper, and doesn't feel it necessary to appear old. The *Dispatch* could be locked into old Hiram's will, which maybe says that the outside of the paper can never be changed (the insides have pictures and modern, wider columns) and that his personally devised system of counting volumes must always be used. I still don't know how old the *Dispatch* is, though. And the only real difference I notice in the papers is that one comes in the morning and the other in the afternoon. Let's call it even.

My copy of the *York Daily Record* featured a story about road kills. It was on page 1B, the front page of the Living section (Comics-TV-Movies). A spooky illustration covered four columns and most of the top half of the page. The view is from ground level, looking down the road toward the dark city skyline, across the mushed carcass of a cute little bunny rabbit:

> "The jogger's feet beat rhythmically against the
> roadside gravel as he settled into the evening run.
> Stars sparkled...Crisp air pervaded...
>
> "It was a glorious night to be alive.
>
> "But not everything was.
>
> "There, under a street light, lay a fresh road kill. A light-brown rabbit thrown into the runner's path as it bounced off the tire of a car."

There followed an investigation of sorts conducted by the reporter (the jogger?) concerning responsibility for pooper-scooping the flattened fauna out of the jogger's path. Telephone calls were made to city, county and state offices, but nobody came forward to claim dead meat as part of his or her job. The reporter seemed to think the buck (no pun intended) was being passed around. But there would be no crime exposed, and certainly no unsung County Carcass Cleanup Crew; it seems the taxpayers never felt it necessary to fund such a thing. Not quite 3,000 words later the reporter trots off into the sunset, resigned to the bald truth that maggots and buzzards will have to continue picking up where Monsieur Michelin leaves off.

Last but not least I should mention "Delaware's Largest Selling Weekly Newspaper," *The Whale*, "Serving Saltwater Sussex County." Each section has a whale and a wavy water line across the top. On the front page the whale beckons in a cartoon bubble: "Get shovels in hand to build castles in the sand."

Diners

Just north of Westfield, Massachusetts, is a squat, dreary building standing alone in a pool of parking lot. Most of the outside walls are covered with a tired red siding, which I presumed had something to do with the name of the place, the Redwood Restaurant I think it is, although I never found out for sure. A sign points to the bar and game room around back, but every patron I saw headed for the lunch counter, or a booth if one was free. I took a small table by a window.

It was Valentine's Day. The cold heart of New England winter had smothered everything with at least three feet of snow; some of the plowed walls along the road were taller than Stan the Van. The temperature was locked in single

digits, and Stan, bless his lousy little heating system, was totally incapable of keeping me warm. My toes felt like piano keys in an ice box. It was time for a hot meal with dignity, something with more presence, more stucco, than franchised food: It was time for a bowl of able-bodied, homemade clam chowder. The crowd of local cars, pickups and delivery trucks told me I could get it at the Redwood.

Sure enough, chowder was the specialty, brewed fresh every day by one of the owners, a big, pleasant woman who kept up a steady conversation with folks at the counter. She left sandwiches, grinders and other standard fare to the cook in the kitchen, a lanky guy who was friendly but not a talker. Her job seemed to be chat, chowder and cash register.

The chowder was proud stuff. Chunks of potato and plenty of clam bits in a thick, creamy soup that steamed against the window. I broke up all my crackers into the broth, in pieces not so small they wouldn't hold a crunch when I spooned them out. A grilled cheese sandwich, milk and coffee rounded out the meal, and everything got warm and happy down inside my flannel shirt. My toes got happy too.

Now that I was comfortable I took a second cup of coffee, leaned back in my seat, and watched as customers came in all hunched from the cold. Most of them ordered chowder, and soon enough peeled away hats and scarfs and sweaters. The place filled up and little snatches of many conversations bounced around the room. It was a nice place to be, watching people get feeling good.

At the height of the lunchtime rush, when the counter and the booths were full and the talking and the clatter of dishes seemed to thicken the air and a line of folks holding coats stood waiting to pay their checks, a tall girl about 20 hurried in from the frigid weather clutching a bunch of red and white helium balloons. The balloon strings were tied together with red ribbon and the girl's lips were smeared with glistening red lipstick. She asked for the cook and the big woman hollered for him through the swinging kitchen door.

The girl was wearing a heavy winter coat, ear muffs and gloves, but she didn't have anything on her legs except pantyhose. She wore heeled boots that might have been red once, a long time ago. Around the top they had a broad, furry strip that once had been white. She held an envelope in one hand and the balloons in the other, which made it difficult unbuttoning her coat, the balloons bouncing against her face and the envelope getting bent. All she had on beneath the coat was a sequined tank suit, red again, lined with more furry strips. The ear muffs had crushed the bunny ears on her head.

Things had quieted down. The cook came out just as the girl got her coat undone.

"Do you want me to take this off?" she asked him. She meant the coat but was feeling in the air above her head for the ears.

"No, that's OK," he said. He wanted to go back to his sandwiches.

The Valentine's Day love bunny handed the cook the envelope. He opened it and read the card inside. She tried to plant a big, shiny red smooch on his lips but his frozen stance and red face made him look like a stop sign, so she just gave him a polite peck and handed him the balloons. He acted like the whole affair was his execution. He turned and disappeared through the swinging door, trailing the balloons. The balloons got caught. There was a groan from the kitchen side, and then, with a big tug, the whole bunch vanished and the door swung shut.

It seemed the girl had enjoyed the presentation about as much as the cook had. She didn't even button up before ducking back out into the cold. She sure could have used a little chowder.

For those of you lamenting the disappearance of roadside diners and small home-style restaurants, I have good news: They are alive and well all over the northeast. These places are refreshingly void of all the fashionable fare so popular in urban and suburban restaurants. Sometimes, just reading the menu would give a nutritionist a case of the vapors. But

you're not here to perpetuate the current pop vitamin; you're here to chow down. Just so the plate is full and the coffee's hot.

Here's a brief survey of some nice, honest eatin' spots:

The Hightstown Diner in Hightstown, New Jersey, offers "pencil points" (pasta cut at an angle and covered with a thick tomato sauce) and taxi service. I shouldn't jump to conclusions, but the tables full of New Jersey Turnpike employees seem to say all that's necessary about what they think of Big Boy and Roy Rogers franchise menus.

At the Bun 'N Cone in Margaretville, New York, autumn conversation hangs on two topics: Who's workin', and Got your deer yet? You get Two Eggs any style, a pile of Home Fries, Toast, three pieces of Ham (or bacon), unlimited coffee and an earful of local news for only two and a half bucks.

At tiny Stemie's Restaurant just north of Riegelsville, Pennsylvania, muddy softball players sit next to Shriners in tuxedos sitting next to mom and three pogo-jumpy kids. Next to them is a shunpiker staring at a poster of John Wayne, The Duke. Service is slow today because the waitress is busy holding hands with her boyfriend across the counter. Burgers are sizzling, coffee is perking, toast is ready to pop.

I arrived moments late to get the last crab cake sandwich at the Conowingo Diner in Conowingo, Maryland. The owner asked if I was in a hurry. No, I wasn't. It'll take him 15 minutes to make some more—can I wait? Sure thing. I perused the selections on the booth jukebox. An old sign over the counter illustrated First Aid For Choking. That's no reflection on the crab cake sandwich. Even the waitress who brought it lit up with "Hmm, looks good!"

The menu said "New England's Finest Dining Car," but they were out of chowder when I stopped at Zip's in Dayville, Connecticut. But how could I be disappointed? On the roof, atop a three-sided aluminum tower, the word EAT is proclaimed to all the world in ruby neon. The waitresses—there were no waiters—were all dressed in perfect white uniforms with red aprons, tied in back with big floppy bows. They all wore white shoes. And curiously, they all stood almost exactly the same height.

"Are you serving lunch yet?"
"Breakfast, lunch, dinner, you name it," she said.
Then she scrubbed my formica booth table 'til it squealed.

X Marks the Spot

For the young at heart and the old enough, shunpiking offers something turnpikes and cities can't—privacy in a rural setting. This is important for anyone in love or working at it: No romance can be expected to flower without a little room to breathe. Somewhere out there, down a lightly traveled, curvy road, a sun-buttered meadow awaits you and your sweetie. Or maybe it's a high rock overlooking the valley. A clearing in the woods. A barn full of hay, freshly cut. The bees buzz, the streams gurgle and the birds birdle. That's how it is with love. Don't forget the blanket, the bordeaux, and the bread and cheese.

These love spots are not shown on any map. But if your mind is on the subject, you'll find something. Mark it with an X for future reference.

A Few Words From Our Special Guest

"There's real life for you...the open road, the dusty highway, the heath, the common, the hedgerows, the rolling downs! Camps, villages, towns, cities! Travel, change, interest, excitement! The whole world before you, and a horizon that's always changing! The real way to travel! The only way to travel! O bliss! O poop-poop! O my! O my!"

MR. TOAD
The Wind in the Willows

Hopping State Lines

Mr. Toad, the star of Kenneth Grahame's classic tale *The Wind in the Willows*, was one of the world's first great shunpikers. He was constantly veering off the beaten path to experience new places and things, which frequently led him to wild adventure, and sometimes danger.

In Toad's honor, today's shunpikers symbolically hop across state lines by performing the Toad Memorial Hop, known also as the *Toad-Hop*.

Here's how it's done:

Whether you are paying tribute to The Flag, your mother's cooking, a one-night stand or Mr. Toad, your behavior should be at all times proper when the tribute is being offered. In the case of the *Toad-Hop*, this involves an honorable shunpiking state of mind and all four appendages (hands and feet).

As you near a state border, keep an eye out for a change in the road surface. This is the actual state line. It may be from blacktop to concrete or vice versa. Even if the road material is the same on both sides of the line, one side is usually darker because that state resurfaced its share of the road more recently than the other.

As you cross the line, remain in your seat but raise your

knees in the air and your hands about head high. Point your toes straight to the ground, as if you depended on that extra effort to reach a lily pad, and extend your fingers to full length, spread as far apart as possible. Repeat with obvious enthusiasm Toad's immortal words: "O Bliss! O poop-poop! O my! O my!" Ideally, the hop will be timed so you cross the line right when you get to the hyphen in "poop-poop."

(Note: Signs that welcome you into the great state of so-and-so are almost always well beyond the actual state line. Use the sign as a state line designation only if you have missed the change in the road surface. There is one exception to this: When the state line runs along a river or down its main channel, a welcome sign, or even one that says plainly State Line, should be used. If there is no sign on the bridge, jump off the bridge onto the shore when you reach the new state.)

In performing the *Toad-Hop*, drivers get a rare opportunity to pay homage with panache. Mindful of driving safety, it is easy enough to keep a few finger tips on the wheel. The sign of a truly artful *Toad-Hop* is, however, demonstrated by one's ability to maintain speed, the tip of the right foot keeping steady pressure on the gas pedal even though the heel is above the toe. A tribute paid jerkily is tantamount to batting a beach ball during the national anthem, and one achieved through the use of cruise control is no tribute at all. It's blasphemy.

The Shunpiker's Prayer*

O spirit Hula Doll
Shake them grassy hips
And help us to avoid
Turnpikes on our trips.

*This solemn offering is most effective if recited while Hula Doll dances. Just flip the upper right-hand corners of these pages, say the words, and your prayer will be answered.

The Shunpikes

An Important Note, Especially for Southbound Shunpikers

Each of these shunpikes consists of a loosely descriptive introduction followed by detailed directions. In an effort to minimize confusion in the introductions, sights are described in the order they would be encountered traveling northward.

The directions are also presented south to north. They are divided into numbered Legs, Leg 1 always at the southern end and the last Leg always the northernmost. A shunpiker going north from Washington to Boston would begin with Leg 1, proceeding to Legs 2, 3 and so on. *In coming south from Boston to Washington, shunpikers must remember to progress backwards through the directions, that is, from Leg 6 to Leg 5 to Leg 4, etc., down to Leg 1.* Since a right turn going north becomes a left turn going south, and vice versa, each Leg includes directions for both north- and southbounders to keep things as clear as possible.

Perhaps you southbound shunpikers are wondering why you get the honor of following directions backwards and reading descriptions that have to be remembered backwards. You deserve an explanation:

My three brothers all attended famous institutions of higher learning in Boston. They then went out into the world and got jobs that require snap judgment and regular haircuts.

Consequently, they speak with authority, even when they're full of hooey. Each of them sits at a desk in the middle of an office and faces the door like a gunfighter. They don't turn their backs on anyone. They go to meetings in faraway places.

Whether or not I ask for it, my dear brothers are forever impressing me with how much they know, and I must admit that all in all they are pretty darn smart. I think it has something to do with their enlightened schooling in Boston.

When it came time to present these shunpikes on paper in a book, I was faced with a tricky format problem. I couldn't figure out how to present both the going north and the going south at the same time. My brothers say it's because these directions are "linear." What they mean, I think, is that you can't describe both ends of a line at the same time. So I had to make a choice: Arrange things either going north or going south.

Although my brothers are quite brilliant, I wouldn't say they are unique. I mean, Boston's institutions surely have turned out a lot more than these three wizards. So I'm guessing that the brilliance factor—my brothers like to "factor" things—is pretty strong up around Boston. I factored that into my decision. These shunpikes are arranged from south to north because my brothers have convinced me that people up north going south can figure things out.

The Jersey Surprise Shun

*************** *****************

*Avoid the reeking herd,
Shun the polluted flock.*

ELINOR HOYT WYLIE

When I was a college student in West Germany, I went on a trip with a busload of other students to Prague, the millenia-old capital of Czechoslovakia. For most of us it was our first visit to a communist country. At the German-Czech border we all handed in our passsports for stamping, and stood around talking seriously about communism and our forthcoming dinner stop in Pilsen, where the beer is made the way everybody likes it—the Bohemian way.

A friend of mine named Fritz fell into conversation with a woman border guard. She asked him if he had ever visited Czechoslovakia.

"I've been to Moscow and Leningrad," he said.

The guard could hardly contain her rage. Firmly and clearly she spoke, so not to be misunderstood.

"This is NOT Russia!" she said.

Poor Fritz. All his life he'd been taught to think of Iron Curtain countries as one big pile of commies. Whether they were called Poles, Czechs, Hungarians or whatever else wasn't supposed to matter. But it did. His blunder was in thinking they were all Russians, and the border guard was furious about it.

As a result, Fritz was the only one of us not admitted to the country. The official reason for the rejection was a discrepancy between his passport photo and his actual ap-

pearance. The photo showed a mustache, but he was currently clean shaven. It was a judgment call, with the guard as judge. He was sent back. (Later, with the help of a sympathetic German barkeeper, Fritz glued some of his curly red locks to his upper lip and tried again. He made it through with his fake mustache, but had to hitchhike to join us in Prague and missed that wonderful Pilsener beer.)

Now imagine this conversation between a turnpiker and a New Jersey native:

"Have you ever been to New Jersey?" the native asks the turnpiker.

"I've been to the Vince Lombardi Service Area on the Turnpike," the turnpiker answers.

The Jersey native can hardly contain his rage. Firmly and clearly he speaks, so not to be misunderstood.

"The Turnpike is NOT New Jersey!"

Poor turnpiker. All his life he's been taught that New Jersey is nothing but a turnpike. Aside from slot machines and the stench of the Meadowlands, he has no idea what lies beyond the Asphalt Curtain.

If he would only try the Jersey Surprise Shunpike he'd see what he's been missing.

One of the great pleasures I took in prowling around the Northeast looking for shunpikes was discovering the *rest* of New Jersey. Believe it or not, New Jersey has the third largest state park system in the country. Not bad for the fifth smallest state. Each spring the one-day Audubon Society bird count totals nearly 250 species. Almost a hundred battles of the American Revolution were fought here, and George Washington and his Continental Army spent a full third of the war in New Jersey, longer by far than in any other state. Woodrow Wilson, who cleaned up New Jersey politics when he was governor, loved to ride his bicycle here. And about New Jersey's nickname, "the Garden State": When you're mired in the rank cesspool of north Jersey's freeway traffic, it's hard to believe a New Jersey garden could be anything more than a limp bouquet on a tombstone. Yet wandering around the state's *rural* areas (yes, rural is a word used in New Jersey) during growing season you'll see acres of blueberries, raspberries, strawberries and even cranberries; apple and peach orchards; vineyards; tomatoes on top of tomatoes; watermelons; lettuce, cabbage and spinach; potatoes and sweet potatoes. There are probably more flowers for sale at Jersey roadside stands than fruits and vegetables.

Like George Washington, I spent more time wandering around and camping in New Jersey than in any other state during my shunpiking research campaign, partly because it happens to lie midway between Washington and Boston so I passed through a lot, but also because it's a nice place to be. After a while I began to think that everybody in the state with a spare piece of ground had something growing in it, especially mums. My favorite stretch is the area from Trenton north along, and inland east from, the Delaware River. That's where this Shunpike takes you. Enjoy the road; most New Jersey tourists are on the Atlantic beaches, so you don't have to worry about rude mobs here.

The Jersey Surprise Shunpike abandons traditional northeast corridor traffic outside Washington, D.C., running instead over to the Eastern Shore of Maryland and Delaware. The shun joins turnpike traffic to cross the Delaware Memorial Bridge and meanders briefly through south Jersey before cutting through a corner of Pennsylvania. It passes Washington Crossing and follows the Delaware River north; veers away to explore the rural uplands of central and northwestern New Jersey; crosses the Hudson and the Taconic Range into the rugged northwestern corner of Connecticut; and then scoots through the dense woodlands of central and eastern Massachusetts before meeting Boston's I-495.

Those of you coming north from Richmond pass through Fort A. P. Hill before crossing the Potomac into Maryland. About eight miles east of Bowling Green and three miles west of Port Royal, still within the army base, is a marker on the left indicating the site of the Garrett Farm (it can only be seen from the northbound side of the divided four-lane). John Wilkes Booth, who had assassinated President Lincoln 12 days earlier, was cornered and killed in a barn here before dawn on April 26, 1865.

If you've spent years battling I-95 traffic between Richmond and the Delaware Memorial Bridge, you'll be dumbstruck when you discover the serenity you could have had all along by cruising the wide open roads on the Eastern Shore (the broad peninsula that lies between the Chesapeake Bay and the Atlantic). Your route is bordered by farmland stretching out in every direction, populated mostly by flocks of red-winged blackbirds. It is a little like traveling a road on the Great Plains; the sheer vastness is such a pleasure I often finding myself slowing down just to prolong the experience.

Once across the Delaware Memorial Bridge the route turns away from the New Jersey Turnpike, simply to prove that New Jersey has its charms. Just west of Woodstown on US40 is Cowtown, where huge statues of a cowboy and a steer invite you to come to the rodeo every summer Saturday night at 7:30. "Often Imitated, Never Equalled," says the sign. I'd love to hear a bronco buster in chaps with a thick north Jersey accent. Imagine the campfire songs: "Er, gimme a herm, where da berffeller rerm. . ." I don't think that's quite it. How about, "Seldom is hoid, a discoiragin' woid. . ." That's better.

You can see brahma bulls, or steers, or whatever, in small pens just on the east edge of Woodstown. The town itself is very quaint, with tree-lined streets and some well-kept Victorian buildings, including the prominent stone First National Bank. But the real sight to see in Woodstown is Erdner's Busy Corner, on NJ45 just north of town. As I understand it, a fellow named Erdner built up this impressive truck-farming operation, which serves the local growers and stockmen. After achieving some success and community prominence, Mr. Erdner apparently felt a need to deliver a message, perhaps his secrets of success, or was simply overcome by a desire to fill in all the blank spaces on his half dozen long, white, mostly windowless warehouses. Whatever the reason, the urge resulted in a kind of epigrammatic festooning of the buildings. That is, the warehouses now serve as billboards for Erdner's busy answers to questions nobody ever asks. And dangling words of wisdom, even on a warehouse, warranted something better than U-Pick-Em lettering. Many are painted in an elegant black script reminiscent of the first moments of old movies, when a dusty book cover would open with "Once upon a time. . ." and tell you the background of the tale you were about to see. Some of the sayings are in quotation marks, and since they're big enough to be read a hundred yards away they seem to carry extra weight, as if they were handed down like commandments by you know who. They weren't.

When I first saw Erdner's Busy Corner and the wisdom on the walls, I pulled in where the sign said "Saws Sharpened Here" to pick up a few tips. After all, you never know when your life might become a garden state of rotten fruit.

I looked up and beheld these words:

There are only two kinds of people: those who realize what's the matter with them and those who don't.

They struck me as *words to live by*, if you want to know the truth. I made a quick check and figured I fit in with the latter bunch, the don't-knows, and decided my driving time could be well spent working my way into the other bunch, which I gathered was the preferred place to be. Then I read this:

> The difference between you and other people is that their money looks bigger and their troubles smaller.

I was a little confused. From reading the first saying, I thought the world was divided into what's-the-matter knows and what's-the-matter don't-knows. Now I had to figure out where this new information fit in. Right when I'd got it worked out, that I was a what's-the-matter don't-know with small money, and therefore big troubles, I went and read another wall, a big mistake:

> Whatever you may be sure of, be sure of this; that you are dreadfully like other people.

Well, shit. Why should I knock myself out trying to become a what's-the-matter know with big money and small troubles if all it'll get me is a lousy personality?

I was beginning to get a little ticked off when I came upon:

> Every sixty seconds you are angry you lose a full minute of happiness.

I thought of asking some of the employees for advice on interpreting these things, but dropped the idea when I saw:

> Advice is seldom welcome. Those who need it most like it least.

I saw a couple of men filling a pickup with sacks of fertilizer or some such thing. Keeping my quandary to myself, I asked them about Erdner. Turns out he had died the week before. "What kind of person was he?" A long pause. One of the men finally said this much: "It's not good to be saying things about a man after he's passed on."

Employees who kept silent for fear of stirring the wrath of a dead man's ghost. Now how could that happen to somebody full of so much wisdom?

Happiness is a perfume you cannot pour on others without getting a few drops on yourself.

Maybe Erdner wasn't much for opening the perfume bottle.

Rise to the occasion but know when to sit down.

Was he standing on everybody's toes?

To those who talk and talk, this adage doth appeal; the steam that blows the whistle will never turn the wheel.

Maybe his employees were just applying this one to their daily work. Keep your mouth shut and keep the wheel turning.

It occurred to me that maybe I wasn't cut out to make it in Erdner's world.

Success is a ladder which cannot be climbed with your hands in your pockets. Stopping at third base adds nothing to the score. Go all the way.

As I was leaving, and starting to have doubts about my gumption to accept Erdner's challenge, I read this one:

Keep your face to the sunshine and you will not see the shadows.

I don't know what it means, but I rode off into the sunset

and didn't look back, and I have yet to run into any potholes on the shunpiker's highway of life. (I think it's catching.)

Some of New Jersey's gardens can be seen north of Woodstown; there's the "Horspital" too. After Mullica Hill the New Jersey Turnpike is used to get through the congestion of Philadelphia suburbs. When you get off the Turnpike and go into Burlington, check your appetite. The Burlington Diner, on US130 in Burlington, is a classic old diner where business is just as good now as it's ever been. Your waitress might sling the food, walk across the street to the gas station to inspect the transmission work being done on her car, then return and ask if you'd like more coffee. Meanwhile the owner sneaks a piece of pie out of the cooling case.

Here's a takeoff for a friendly argument: Would there be the town and the well-preserved sites of Washington Crossing if Emanuel Leutze had *not* painted *Washington Crossing the Delaware?* Do we visit this place to commemorate the event, or to see where the event that inspired the painting took place? Don't say both—that'll fizzle the whole exercise. Pick an attitude and duke it out. Who knows, you might happen upon a *revelation,* and that could get the discussion really out of hand. Youngest in the car is appointed referee. All decisions by the referee are final.

For those of you who need background, Washington Crossing is the site where George Washington's struggling Continental Army staged its 1776 Christmas night crossing of the Delaware River to surprise the Hessians quartered at Trenton. The Hessians were routed, and Washington's men gained some confidence to continue the fight for independence.

Leutze, who grew up on the banks of the Delaware down river, specialized in dramatic "ten-acre tapestries," and his huge, stirring depiction of Washington's daring attack has been an American favorite ever since its completion in 1851. There is a reproduction at the visitor center in Pennsylvania (Leutze's masterpiece is probably the most widely reproduced American painting *ever*).

Northbounders who want to go through Washington Crossing should take the last Pennsylvania exit off I-95 before entering New Jersey and then turn left to meet up with PA532 and a right-hand turn to the town. Also, if you've heard that New Hope, Pennsylvania, is just a darling place to shop even though you can't find a parking place on warm sunny weekends, you can follow the west bank of the Delaware River north from Washington Crossing to get there. In the route directions, I take you over to the New Jersey side for the trip along the river because the road is more open. Both sides are beautiful, though, and if you simply feel like it, six bridges allow you to zig-zag back and forth across the river as you work your way along between I-95 and Frenchtown, New Jersey.

A note to southbounders concerning Washington Crossing: The road that runs south from PA532 down to the I-95 interchange is not numbered. A simple way to get to I-95 without getting lost is to cross over to the New Jersey side and run south on NJ29 (the route described in the directions); or you can ask the folks at the Washington Crossing visitor center how to go on the Pennsylvania side.

On a New Jersey hill (Goat Hill) that rises above the Delaware River valley and NJ29 at Lambertville is a huge rock that affords a sweeping view across the river toward New Hope, Pennsylvania. In the early part of December, 1776, George Washington looked out over the Delaware from this rock and was pleased to see that a large fleet of boats collected by his Continental Army was safely hidden from view. Having taken several lickings at the hands of

Lord Cornwallis and the mighty British army, Washington had retreated across the river into Pennsylvania to regroup. He had assembled the boats needed for a return to New Jersey and now gambled that Cornwallis would shortly be standing on this same rock looking for signs of the fleet. Satisfied that his deception would work, Washington crossed back to Pennsylvania to rejoin his men. Cornwallis arrived in pursuit of the Americans a few days later. In response to rumors about the rowboat armada, British soldiers were sent up to the rock to search for boats. Like Washington, they saw nothing. Cornwallis dismissed the rumor, and the gamble had paid off. Three weeks later the Americans crossed back over the river and whipped the Hessians at Trenton, Leutze created the national anthem on canvas, and the historic promontory you pass under became known as Washington's Rock.

After following the river course up to Frenchtown, the route turns inland from the river to traverse gorgeous farm country all the way to the New York border. Here and there are streams begging to be fished.

Just south of Clinton, on the last hill before NJ513 descends into town, you will pass through property that my great-great-great-grandparents Hugh and Mary Exton began farming in 1796. They had left "the tyrants of England," as Hugh put it, to settle in the newly independent United States. Aside from the political attitude suggested by that one comment (in a diary he kept during the Atlantic crossing), Hugh's reasons for coming were purely pragmatic, so far as I know. He was leasing farmland from a difficult landlord in England; in America he could own a farm outright. He was 45 at the time, and Mary 38, with six children. They sold most of what they had—farm equipment, livestock, household goods—and bought 739 acres draping the hill between Pittstown and Clinton. Hugh quickly built a local reputation for his cheesemaking and fine English-bred sheep. The farm isn't much now, but you can easily spot the tree-lined drive at the crest of the hill that leads west to the old house from NJ513. I have heard that a developer is going to build cluster homes here.

I mention all this because I never would have discovered any of it had it not been for shunpiking. A lot of luck (fate?) was involved—Stan the Van happened to break down here—but I surely would not have come upon these family roots had I been confined within the guard rails of an interstate. I nursed Stan to a nearby state park campsite and was put in touch with a guy who too had built a local reputation—for fixing Volkswagens. He needed parts for Stan, however, and this was late on a Friday afternoon, so I settled in to wait until Monday.

I remembered my father talking occasionally of Clinton and early Extons, so with time to kill I began checking stones in the town cemeteries in hopes of discovering some of my kin. These hopes were not especially high. I have always been accustomed to seeing no Extons in graveyards; the name is not common and for several generations now the family has been transient military, living a few years at a time at places all over the globe. Extons are few and scattered.

The first graveyard lived up to my expectations, yielding not a single Exton. I saw plenty of Cregars, though, and that was the Volkswagen repairman's name. For some reason, knowing he had generations of family here gave me confidence that he would do a good job on Stan. He wasn't likely to cheat customers, I thought, especially Cregars, and then pick up and leave town. Roots held him here, and roots would keep him honest. I think there is some truth in this.

The second graveyard seemed even less promising. It was a Presbyterian burying ground, and I had never heard of Presbyterians in the family. Fading sunlight and long shadows made reading the stones difficult, and spotting none of my blood I instead concentrated on trying to pick out oddball inscriptions. But near the back edge of the place, against a wall of corn at least eight feet high, it came at me like a shot: I was suddenly surrounded by Extons. Large family plots full of relatives I had never known existed.

Perhaps you cannot imagine my joy; I find it very hard

to explain, even to myself. I rarely see my name on anything other than mail intended to open my pocketbook. Things that do not last. Here it was scored permanently into large, polished rocks, marble and granite, EXTON in tall block letters. I had never felt such a strength of belonging. It must have been a curious sight, a grown man darting around a graveyard in the twilight, acres of tall, thick corn behind. Obviously touched; harmless but don't engage him. I went from stone to stone, trying to memorize every name and lifespan before darkness took over completely. Those five letters, my surname, seen again and again in this place of lives forgotten, were proof of my origin far deeper than the womb. Reading a family tree on paper is nothing. Standing above my ancestors' bones was a confirmation of life.

I cannot say that I suddenly felt myself an important part of ancient earth or anything like that. All my life I have wanted to know a place, a permanent place, where I could belong. I had just found it.

I later learned that I had been camping on Hugh and Mary Exton's second farm, where they had moved in 1811, and which had been divided among the Exton sons when Hugh died. Now it is mostly under the reservoir water of Spruce Run State Park, but I can accept that. The State of New Jersey preserves this old Exton property. I can go any time and camp and walk on the land of my forebears, and developers cannot reach it.

Mr. Cregar did do a good job on Stan the Van. He let me help out in the work too, and volunteered tips on how best to care for my auto. He gave me a tour of his shop, which was attached to his home, and showed me a beautiful old BMW that he had just finished refurbishing from top to tires. His nephew, another Cregar, assisted after his classes at the community college. He was sort of an apprentice, enjoyed the work, and respected his uncle. We talked about all kinds of things.

All the way north to New York the Jersey Surprise Shunpike surprises: farmland and forests broken by streams, ponds and lakes. And even though the terrain isn't mountainous, it definitely is not flat. Sometimes the route rides plateaus that give views in every direction, and sometimes it goes up and down through small valleys and gorges. It passes by nearly a dozen state parks and forests, and when it crosses into New York it also crosses the Appalachian Trail.

In New York you will be riding I-84 briefly, just to experience the turnpiker version of Chinese water torture. This interstate is built with sections of concrete, each one separated from the next by a little lump of tar running in a line across the roadway. You will notice it immediately: thdump, thdump, thdump, thdump, thdump. Like the drip, drip, drip of the famous water torture, this unending series of thdumps can drive you clean out of your mind. Evidently turnpikers like it: they keep coming back for more. Perhaps it is a sinister turnpike builder's attempt at brainwashing through hypnosis. Fortunately you won't be on it long enough to get hooked.

I have heard that turnpikers make entertaining use of these thdumps. I'll tell you how. Get your car going an even 60 miles per hour. Count the number of thdumps in a minute. Multiply by 60. Now you have the number of thdumps per hour, provided you keep going 60. Multiply by 24, and then 365, and finally 100. Now you have the number of thdumps per century, provided you keep going 60. Talk to your friends about this. Argue. Split hairs. Those turnpikers sure know how to have fun. (Recently somebody tried to smooth things out by scraping away the tar lumps. Now the road is more ragged than ever, and will probably be resurfaced soon.)

The sign for the Taconic Parkway signals the end of your little sample of the torture. It's amazing the relief one feels simply by finding a smooth, or even irregular, road surface.

When you take US44 into Connecticut the rugged landscape lets you know this is New England. US44 was once a main through route, but it is now left to shunpikers and local travelers. I think it's beautiful anytime of year, but spring is especially appealing, when every other plant along the roadside seems to be a lilac bush, the sweet aroma of their lavender flowers filling the air.

Not long after you cross the Connecticut River in Holyoke, Massachusetts, your route will be enveloped almost continually by forest, especially to the east of Barre. (Getting through Barre is a trip in itself; I explain why in the directions.) Because the east-west flow of MA62 is blocked by the Quabbin Reservoir, which stretches across the middle third of the state's north-south breadth, few people use this road. It's all yours, so take it away!

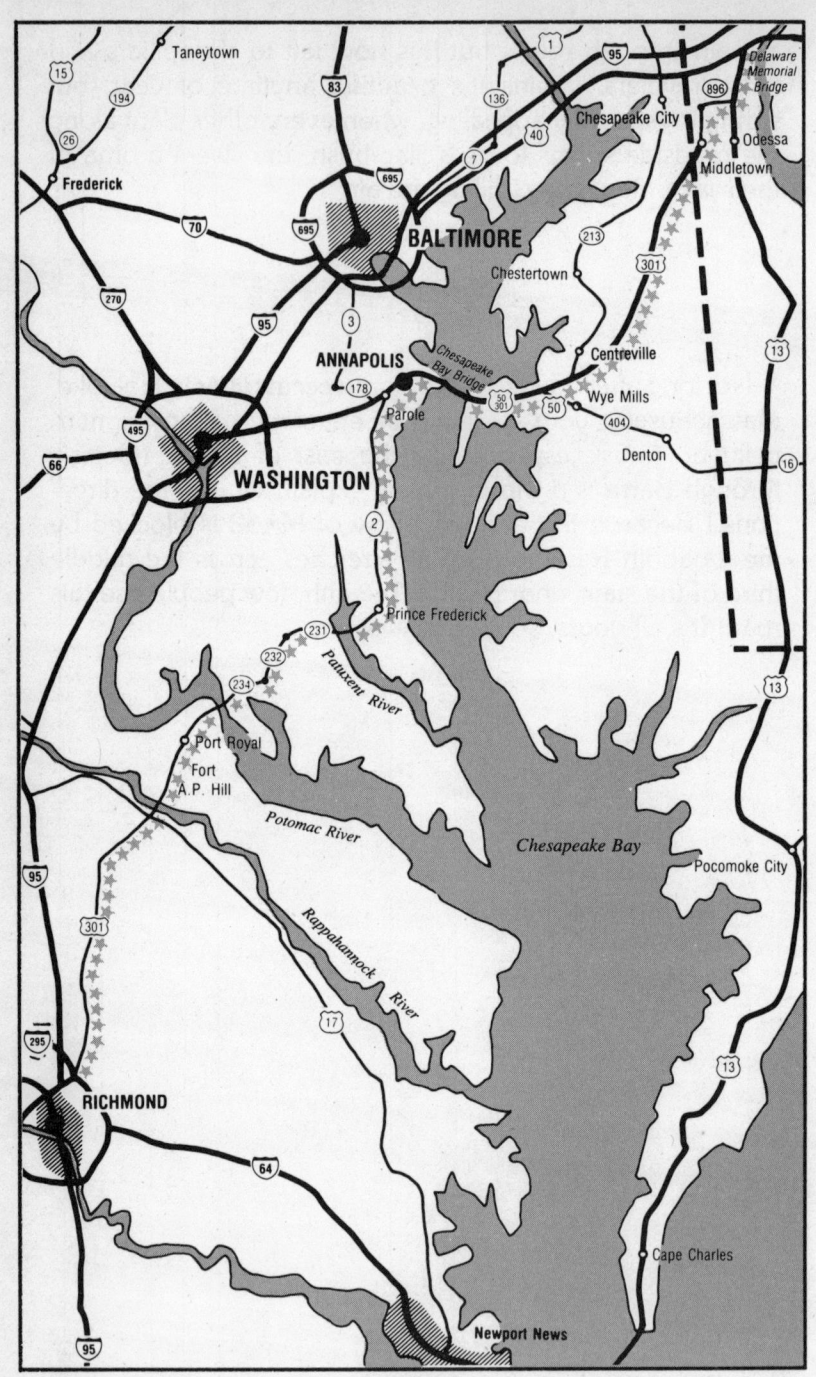

Jersey Surprise Shun: Legs 1 and 2

Directions: Jersey Surprise Shun
Approximately 535 miles, Washington to Boston

Leg 1
Richmond, Virginia, to Annapolis, Maryland

Northbound

Route Sequence:
US301—
MD234—
MD232—
MD231—
MD2—
US50/301

Take US301 north from Richmond through the army base Fort A.P. Hill (watch for the marker locating the Garrett Farm, about two miles west of Port Royal), and cross the Potomac River. About 3 miles after the Potomac bridge you'll see the old White House Motel. Turn right immediately after the motel onto MD234 and go five miles to a left turn onto MD232. When MD232 meets MD231, go right with MD231. Continue across MD5 on MD231, cross the Patuxent River and turn left onto MD2 in Prince Frederick. Be alert for the fork when MD2 splits with MD4 at All Saints Church (under the trees on the hill). Take MD2 north to Parole; follow signs for US50/301, which takes you to the Bay Bridge.

Southbound

Route Sequence:
US50/301—
MD2—
MD231—
MD232—
MD234—
US301

Once you get across the Bay Bridge you have about six miles on US50/301 before you exit at Parole onto MD2. Don't be confused by the signs for MD2 going north to Glen Burnie; wait until you cross the Severn River and pass the signs for the Annapolis exits. Follow MD2 signs out of Parole and go south to Prince Frederick, where you take MD231, a right turn. MD231 becomes MD232; that's what you want until a right turn onto MD234. Go left onto US301, cross the Potomac and follow US301 all the way to Richmond.

Leg 2
Bay Bridge (MD) to Delaware Memorial Bridge (DE-NJ)

Northbound

Route Sequence:
US50/301—
US301
 (MD213—
 MD290—
 US301)—
DE896—
US13/301

Off the Bay Bridge, accompany all the US50 beach traffic until you bear left when US301 parts company with US50. US301 takes you all the way to Middletown, DE, unless you want to vary your route by taking MD213 (see description in Variation 2), a left turn five miles after leaving US50. (MD213 rejoins US301 by taking MD290 east at Galena.) In Middletown US301 traffic is directed around town by a left turn and then a right at DE896. If you prefer seeing Middletown and Odessa, just continue straight and you'll meet up with US13. Both ways make a left once you hit US13. Continue north until you join I-295 running north to the Delaware Memorial Bridge.

Southbound

Route Sequence:
US13/301—
DE896—
US301
 (MD290—
 MD213)—
US50/301

A maze of exits and hellbent traffic greet you coming off the Delaware Memorial Bridge. You want US13/301 southbound. A little congestion in the New Castle area soon gives way to open road. US301 traffic is directed to make a right turn onto DE896, a left onto US301 again, and then a right at the light outside Middletown. You can vary this by continuing south to a right turn onto DE299 in Odessa and going through both old towns, where you will be observed by lots of folks on front porch rockers. US301 then takes you south to US50 and the Bay Bridge. (Taking MD290 to MD213 through Chestertown is a nice route also; see description in Variation 2.)

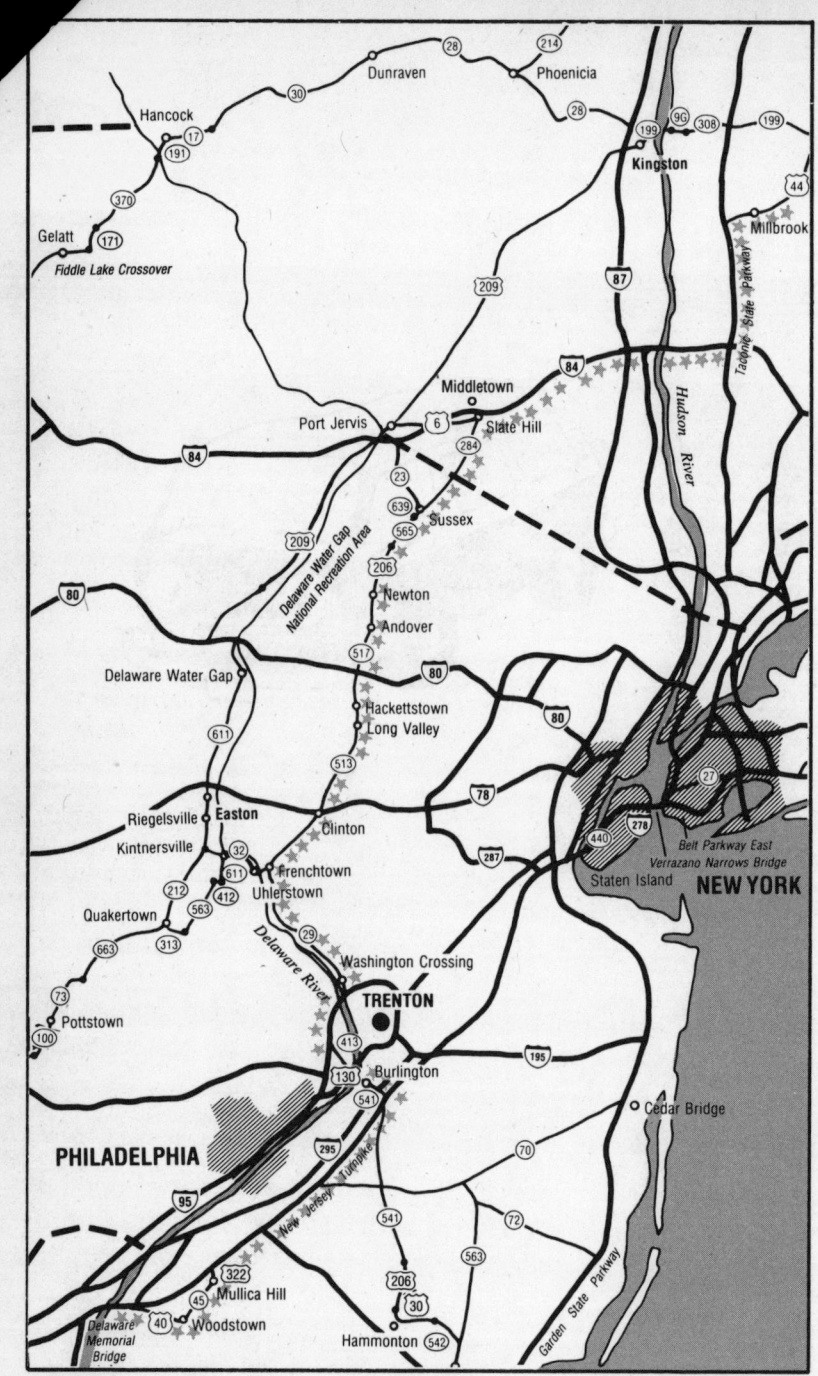

Jersey Surprise Shun: Legs 3 and 4.

Leg 3
Delaware Memorial Bridge to Frenchtown, New Jersey

Northbound

Route Sequence:
US40—
NJ45—
US322—
NJTnpk—
NJ541-Truck—
US130—
PA413—
I-95—NJ29

As you descend off the Delaware Memorial Bridge, keep your eyes open for signs taking you to the right onto US40 east. Ride US40 bareback to Woodstown, NJ, slowing down just before you get there to admire the huge cowboy and steer at Cowtown, New Jersey's version of the Calgary Stampede. In Woodstown turn left (north) onto NJ45. North of town, stop long enough at Erdner's Busy Corner to memorize one of the sayings painted on the buildings. At Mullica Hill go left with NJ45 and then turn left at a stoplight onto US322 westbound. Then run with the livestock on the New Jersey Turnpike north to Exit 5 (Burlington/ Mount Holly). Go left on NJ541 to Burlington, keeping your eyes open for signs to the Burlington-Bristol Bridge. Just as you pass under the I-295 overpass, bear right onto Truck 541 and go straight ahead. This acts as a bypass around some of Burlington. When you get into town take a left where signs for the bridge and Camden tell you to; this is US130, a commercial divided highway. (Unless somebody put one up very recently, there is no sign pointing left for US301.) Within a few blocks (½ mile) a sign for PA413 and the bridge will point you off to the right. Go half way 'round the two traffic circles and continue over the bridge.

Welcome to PA. Did you perform a satisfactory Toad-Hop across the state line? Stay in the center lane when there is one and follow the bridge road (PA413) to a traffic light before an underpass. Here you pick up signs for I-95. Make a left and go straight, holding in the center lane; you are on PA413. Under the bridge and through the stoplight continue straight until the sign for I-95 points you left. Take I-95 north across the Delaware River, then exit immediately down onto NJ29 going north. After Washington Crossing keep going north until NJ29 dead-ends in Frenchtown.

Southbound

Route Sequence:
NJ29—
I-95—
PA413—
US130—
NJ541—
NJTnpk—
US322—
NJ45—
US40

Pick up NJ29 in Frenchtown, a left-hand turn. Just below Washington Crossing get on I-95 southbound. Get off at the fourth exit (PA413—Penndel). After exiting turn left, crossing over I-95, then make a quick right onto PA413 to the Burlington/Bristol Bridge. Signs will guide you. Be prepared for the right turn immediately after you pass under US13. Once over into Burlington go straight (half way around) through the two traffic circles and watch for left turn signs onto US130 North to Mount Holly. Do not take the turn for NJ541 to the NJTnpk. Go to the next light and take a right onto Truck 541. Truck 541 bypasses some of old Burlington, then rejoins NJ541 heading toward Mount Holly and the Turnpike. Go south with the Turnpike herd to Exit 2 (Swedesboro—Chester), get off and go east on US322. At Mullica Hill turn south (right) on NJ45. When you get to Erdner's Busy Corner, pause to soak up some of the wisdom Erdner had painted on his warehouses. In Woodstown take US40 west to the Delaware Memorial Bridge. If it's a summer Saturday you're in luck: the Cowtown rodeo (west of Woodstown on US40) starts at 7:30 P.M. Whoopy-tie-yie-yay. Git along.

Leg 4
Frenchtown, New Jersey, to Middletown, New York

Northbound

Route Sequence:
NJ513—
NJ517—
US206—
NJ565—
NJ639—
NJ284
  (becomes
  NY284)—
US6—
I-84

Take a right when NJ29 ends at Frenchtown. You are now on NJ513, which begins a steady climb up out of the Delaware River valley. Approaching Clinton go straight under the I-78 overpass to the second light and make a left. In case you lose count, this is the first light after you cross a bridge. Go straight out of town and merge with NJ31, but don't get too comfortable there. Several hundred yards ahead turn right; the sign points to High Bridge and Voorhees State Park. There is also a battered sign indicating that you have found NJ513 again. Wind up through High Bridge and past Voorhees State Park and Voorhees High School (on the right). In Long Valley take a left onto NJ517 (the road is also West NJ24). Continue north through Hackettstown, following signs for NJ517. Take a left onto US206 when you meet it in Andover. Go through Newton on US206 (be alert for the route signs around the town square) then go straight on NJ565 when US206 turns left. A couple of miles below Sussex a sign will point to the right for NJ565. Don't turn. Keep going straight on NJ639 past the airfield. Go straight into town, bear right at sign for South NJ23, then make an immediate left turn at a white church onto NJ284. There is a sign. Turn right onto US6 east when NY284 ends, then get onto I-84 east; the route is well marked.

Southbound

Route Sequence:
I-84—
US6—
NY284
 (becomes
 NJ284)—
NJ639—
NJ565—
US206—
NJ517—
NJ24—
NJ513—
NJ29

From I-84 take Exit 3W for US6 and 17M (Middletown—Goshen). Off the interstate, get into your left lane immediately so you can make the well-indicated left turn onto westbound US6. In Slate Hill turn left onto NY284, which carries you into New Jersey. When you get to Sussex follow the signs for the airport and Newton. You will be making a right from NJ284 and then a quick left; the road that takes you south past the airport is NJ639. (I have not sampled the fare at the Airport Diner.) NJ639 puts you on NJ565; follow it until it becomes US206, which takes you through Newton. Pay attention to the US206 signs around the Newton town square. In Andover go right with sign for NJ517, and stay on it through Hackettstown, making sure to go straight (east NJ24; NJ517 doesn't rate a sign here) when NJ57 turns right on the town's south side. A steep descent signals the approach to Long Valley, where you turn right onto NJ513. Past Voorhees State Park you descend through nearly vertical High Bridge, then make a left onto NJ31. Just about the time you get your speed up again, where the green embankment of the Spruce Run Reservoir rises on your right, bear right at a fork with a sign pointing to Clinton. Go to the stoplight and turn right. As you cross the bridge you'll see a sign to reassure you that this is still NJ513. Continue straight out of Clinton on NJ513; in Pittstown be careful to turn right with NJ513 just over the creek bridge. In Frenchtown a green sign on the side of a building points left to NJ29. That means you.

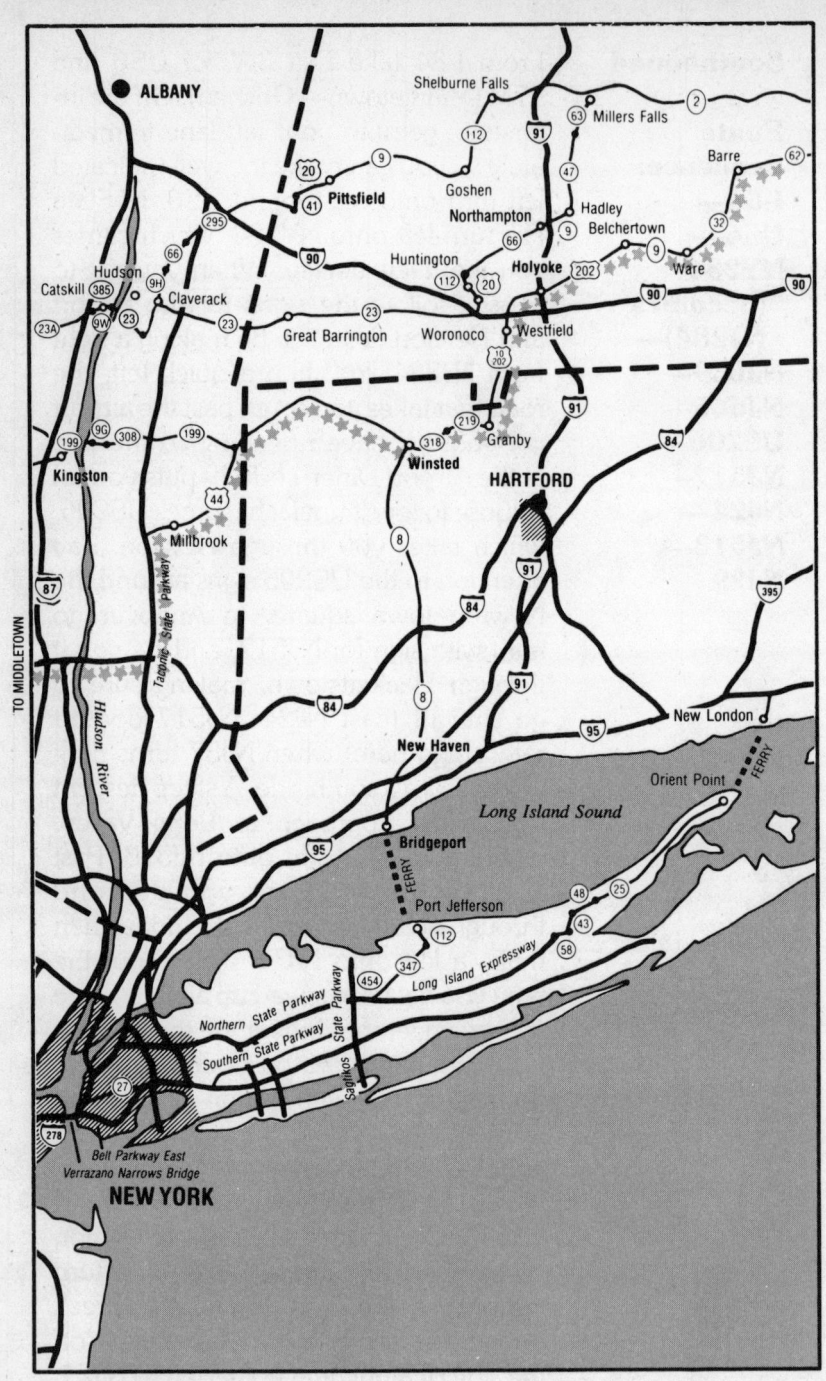

Jersey Surprise Shun: Leg 5.

Leg 5

Middletown, New York, to Westfield, Massachusetts

Northbound

Route Sequence:
I-84—
Taconic
 Parkway—
US44—
CT318—
CT219—
CT20—
CT10/US202

Get off I-84 and go north on the Taconic Parkway as far as US44, which you take eastbound. US44A will take you around Millbrook. US44 is well marked all the way to Winsted, CT. Beyond Winsted to the east, watch for a left turn onto CT318, which runs the gap between Lake McDonough and Barkhamsted Reservoir to join CT219. Take a left onto CT219. Make a hard left when you come to the stoplight in Granby, that puts you on CT10/US202 northbound. Signs for MA10/US202 will guide you through Westfield, MA.

Southbound

Route Sequence:
MA10/US202—
CT20—
CT219—
CT318—
US44—
Taconic
 Parkway—
I-84—
US6

Take MA10/US202 south into Connecticut. At Granby make a hard right at a stoplight to get on CT20 westbound. About three miles west of Granby go left on CT219, go another seven or so miles then make a right onto CT318, which runs between Barkhamsted Reservoir and Lake McDonough. When CT318 ends go right (west) on US44. Follow US44* all the way to the Taconic Parkway, which you take southbound. Go west with I-84 to Exit 3 (US6 and 17M; Middletown—Goshen). Here you pick up US6 West (southbound).

---

*In Winsted, ferrypikers can take CT8 south to Bridgeport Ferry.

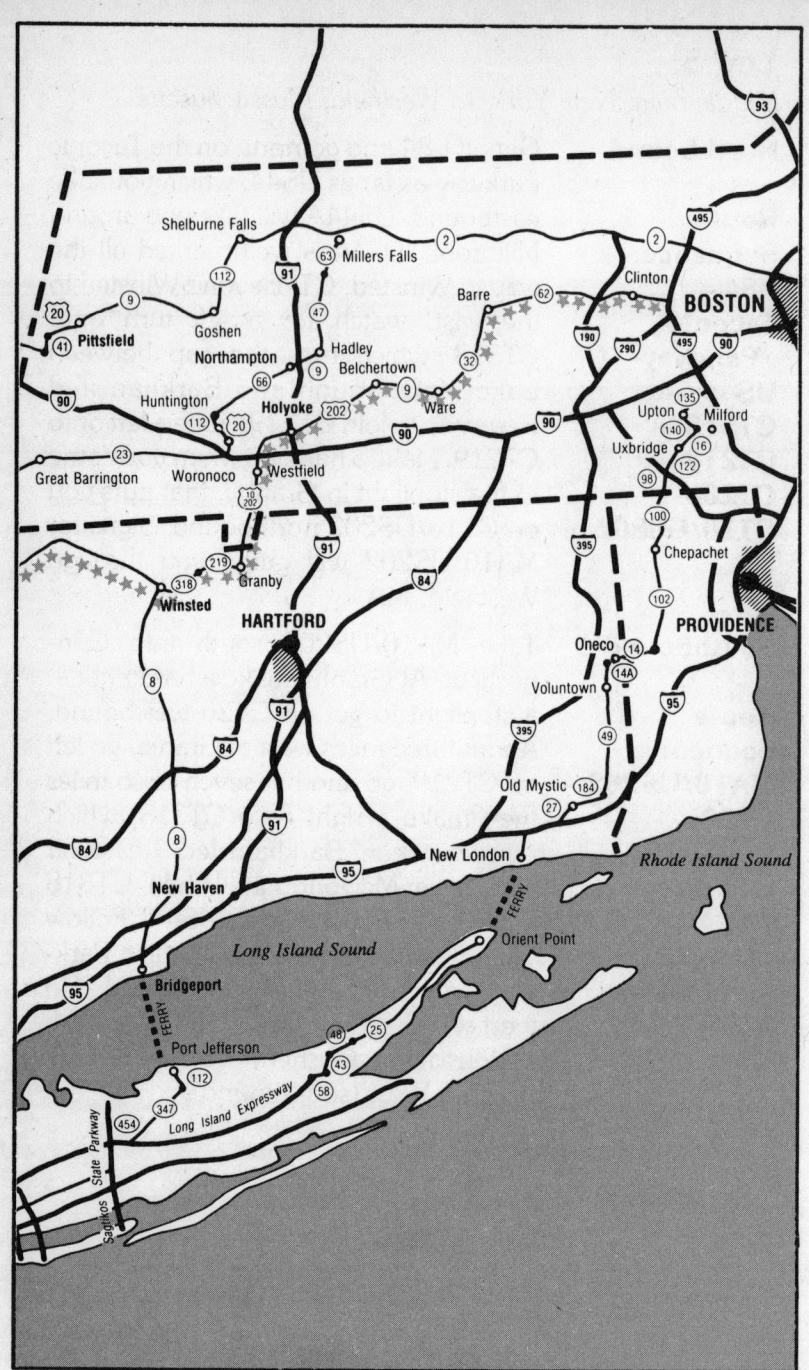

Jersey Surprise Shun: Leg 6.

Leg 6
Westfield, Massachusetts, to Boston's I-495

Northbound

Route Sequence:
US202—
MA9—
MA32—
MA62—
I-495

Continue to follow US202 north of Westfield, turning right when it splits from MA10. The route is well marked through Holyoke, and though it winds around town, you may not have to stop. After crossing the Connecticut River take US202 to Belchertown, where a spur points you right to join MA9 eastbound. In Ware take MA32 north to Barre, and that's where the fun begins. A long incline brings you to the Barre town common, quite large. Pull up along the green and just look around. You can't miss the wonderful old buildings that make up a classic New England town center. After you've admired your surroundings, check out the traffic. Kids flying by helter skelter on skateboards and bikes? Do they weave in and out of cars that come from every direction? Look closely. Do you see one car come down a street on the common one way and then another go up that street, over the same ground, in the opposite direction? I gave up trying to figure what's right and wrong when driving around the Barre town common. I wonder if anybody knows.
In any event, it's now time to push on. Look at the steeples on the town buildings. Find the one with the clock on it, black-faced with Roman numerals (it's got a Paul Revere bell too). A narrow road, practically an alley, leaves the common at the right of the building with the clock steeple. A painted finger on the wall points you to Boston; this is MA62.

Southbound

**Route Sequence:
MA62—
MA32—
MA9—
US202**

Be careful to follow the MA62 signs through Princeton and Clinton.

At Exit 26 head west from I-495 on MA62. You are going to Clinton. Follow the signs through Clinton and be especially careful in Princeton, where a steep incline prevents you from seeing your route signs until the last moment. You come into Barre with very little warning; watch out for the kids darting about on bikes. You should pause to stroll around the common, and you should also orient yourself. Your next route, MA32, descends from the common directly to the left of where you entered, at the end of a row of shops. Take MA32 to Ware and then get on MA9 west. Just beyond Winsor Dam a spur to Belchertown takes you to US202. It is well marked. Follow US202 through Holyoke, a surprisingly pleasant cross-town transit, then join MA10 southbound to Westfield. Signs clearly guide you toward Connecticut.

The Rivers and Ranges ·········· Shun ··········

In a long ramble of the kind on a fine autumnal day, Rip had unconsciously scrambled to one of the highest parts of the Kaatskill mountains. . . . From an opening between the trees he could overlook all the lower country for many a mile of rich woodland. He saw at a distance the lordly Hudson, far, far below him, moving on its silent but majestic course. . . . On the other side he looked down into a deep mountain glen, wild, lonely and shagged.

WASHINGTON IRVING
Rip Van Winkle

Anything could happen on a shunpike that takes you across the Rip Van Winkle Bridge. Several times I have used this bridge over the "lordly" Hudson at the town of Catskill, New York, and with each crossing I have vaguely expected to enter a mist-edged fantasy when reaching the far side. Elves and castles and maidens who need my knightly help. Trees that talk and wizards with moons on their hats. It hasn't happened yet, but knowing I'm in the land of gentle old Rip makes it seem a real possibility. Crossing that bridge and winding up through the Catskill Mountains you too might imagine how Washington Irving's tale could depart reality high in the hazes of their gorgeous clefts.

This shunpike makes a lazy arc through Maryland, Pennsylvania, New York and Massachusetts, around the metropolitan areas that make up the northeast corridor. I call it Rivers and Ranges because those are its primary features; if you want a little wildness and a lot of scenery, this shun fills the bill. It follows the steep forested banks of the Susquehanna River; crosses the northern, less touristed, reaches of the Pocono Mountains; enters the heart of the Catskills, then tops a pass and descends dramatically to the Hudson River; skirts the Berkshire Hills to trace swift rivers and streams along the northern tier of Massachusetts. Perhaps more than two thirds of this shunpike follows waterways large and small (maybe it should be called the Angler's Dream). It is a long shun, about 600 miles between Washington and Boston, but there are lots of places to stay to split it into two comfortable days. And by the time you've completed it you will have seen some of the best scenery in the east. Not only that, you'll have the pleasure of knowing you've avoided about a fifth of the U.S. population.

The southern end of the Rivers and Ranges Shun at Frederick, Maryland, touches the northern tip of the Blue Ridge (and the Shenandoah Valley if you go that way) and crosses the Catoctin Mountains into open Pennsylvania farmland. Above Harrisburg the route passes through a crescent of Appalachian ridges that stretches northeast from south-central Pennsylvania to the Poconos. If you look at a state road map, you can see how those ranges affected road building; the roads run generally east-west through the parallel valleys. For centuries, the best north-south route through these mountains has been the valley of the Susquehanna River, and you will follow this waterway that cuts across the geologic grain from Scranton to Harrisburg, and then gives itself up to the Chesapeake Bay.

At Millersburg, about 20 miles north of Harrisburg, is the last of many ferries that once crossed the Susquehanna. If you want to take the ferry and get a taste of how travel used to go around these parts, I suggest northbounders cross from west to east and southbounders from east to west. This keeps you from running into the ugly congestion along US11 on the west bank of the river at Selinsgrove. On the east bank there isn't a single stoplight along PA147 between your bridges at Clarks Ferry and Sunbury. For several miles along PA147 just north of Clarks Ferry the road is lined with lovely old Sycamore trees, planted by design probably long before the road was ever paved. I suppose that shady stretch of avenue was a once favorite of courting couples who drifted by in slow-moving horse buggies.

The terrain above the Susquehanna toward the northeast corner of the state is characterized by sharp hills and woods that are reminiscent of New England; to me the hills are tight, compact and thick with trees. No wonder Pennsylvania is famous for its hunting and fishing—the deer can hide forever in these woods and there seems to be a trout stream between every ridge. In fact, Pennsylvania has more rivers and streams than any other state.

For those who want to divide the trip into two days and camp for a night, there are 120 campsites at Ricketts Glen State Park west of Scranton and your route, and 96 sites at Lackawanna State Park north of Scranton.

On a brisk November Sunday, my wife and I stopped in for a late lunch at the Cross Country Restaurant, which sits next to a tiny airstrip just south of Tunkhannock on PA29/309. When we walked in it seemed we had made a mistake; most of the formica tables were filled with elderly couples, and all the waitresses were dressed like nurses in uniforms of crinkly white. We thought we had just barged in on the dining room of an old folks home. Except the tables were full of food, heaps of it, not the meager prescription servings for those with the ailments of age. The special was big pieces of chicken on biscuits with gravy, mashed potatoes, beans, corn and a tossed salad—for $5.95. This offering was too sumptuous for some, so half portions were available for

$3.95. Believe me, the tradition of good, starchy grub is alive and well at the Cross Country. It gets you thinking. Maybe the nation grew up big and strong because our fore fathers and mothers packed in lots of meat and potatoes instead of Big Macs and wheat germs. Certainly this room was full of folks named John and Bill and Harry, Mary and Sue and Ruth. A boneless Justin or Shawn, Heather or Kimberly couldn't cut the gravy here. I looked at some of the weathered but hardy old faces and saw soldiers and women who could tame soldiers, workmen and mothers, handshakes and hugs, sorrow and joy and window boxes flowering every spring.

Apparently this gorging on the food that made America strong is a weekly exercise for the older generation around Tunkhannock. (Even the town name is tough enough to whip the Russians.) The people dress up, maybe go to church, and then meet among friends at the Cross Country. My wife and I were not in our church clothes; we found a table and tried to hide our jeans beneath our napkins. We wanted to be sturdy and steady like these folks, so we ordered the food that made America feel great before beer commercials made us look stupid. We were determined to finish the huge portions. Triumphantly we mopped up the last of the gravy with solid biscuits. We drank our milk straight and our honest coffee black. Toothpicks between our teeth, we stepped out into the brisk November day, bellies full and posture proud. All over the country life was simple and good.

The purest bit of shunpiking presented in this book is the Fiddle Lake Crossover, my solution to crossing a tapering shoulder on the northern edge of the Poconos. Even though the roads aren't numbered, this is a very simple, and short, connection between state routes, and it maintains the general direction of the Rivers and Ranges Shun. For a mile or so in the middle, just west of Fiddle Lake, the Crossover glides across high open country; the busy vacation atmosphere of the Poconos to the south and east seems very far away.

Once across the main course of the Delaware River into New York, you run along its East Branch, a great length of which has been dammed as a reservoir to help flush New York City. This brings you into the Catskills, and briefly, to Phoenicia.

This Phoenicia, comfortably tucked under splendid old trees along a babbling trout stream called Esopus Creek, bears absolutely no resemblance to its namesake, the ancient Middle Eastern state that made a name for itself selling fancy whittled tusks all over the Mediterranean back in the B.C. years, when you could be born in the 1900s and die in the 1800s. New York's Phoenicia is different. It has a pleasant main street with some nice houses on it, some of which you'll see if you make a wrong turn at the Phoenicia Pharmacy.

One of these days I'd like to buy the Phoenicia Pharmacy so I can play around with the signs out front. You see, the phirst Phoenicians gave the world the idea of an alphabet, and then some pholks who undoubtedly phelt very indebted named a kind of alphabet in their honor, called phonetics. So, iph there is any place where a store owner should pheel phree to have phun phiddling with spelling and sounds, this little Phoenicia would be it.

As owner, my first move would be to change the neon sign to Foenicia Farmacy. That's pretty tame, and customers probably wouldn't even notice. Those who did might argue that running a half-price sale on trout flies would have got more attention. If I went a little further and made it Funny-Shah Farm-A-Sea, folks would get suspicious of the pharmacist and maybe ask the mayor to run a test on the town water supply. Some of them would go home and read the small print on all the labels in the liquor cabinet, and a few others would come in to buy pilz for a heh-dayk. By the time I got around to using the phonetic spelling found in dictionaries (fi-nē'shə fär'mə-sē), folks would begin to look at familiar words as if they were dangerous objects from another planet. Words like frĕnz and nā'bərz, and spoo'kē pə-jä'məz. They would try to talk but werdz wud get grbld in thayr throwtz. The high school English teacher would be seen milling aimlessly through empty streets and the windows of those nice houses would fill with dark faces peering out. It would be as if the world had mysteriously changed; and then everybody would know just how old Rip felt when he woke up. Wooden chew?

Above Phoenicia the route crosses a notch in the mountains once known as Stony Clove. Ever since Rip's day the Devil has been rumored to live in this "loneliest and most awful corner of the world" that was once a dangerous passage. If your car stalls don't cuss because that just makes the Devil happy. If your prayers are said earnestly he will vanish in the mists and your car will make it smoothly over the pass to begin the descent to the Hudson River. Beware the sound of bowling.

Tannersville is an eponymous reminder of an industry that had a 19th-century heyday all through these mountains: leather tanning. The mountain streams and proximity to transport on the Hudson made this a superb location for turning rough hide into supple leather and then shipping it to markets. Fortunately tanners no longer fell huge stands of trees for the tannin needed to brown hides. Instead, modern entrepreneurs level them for ski runs, like the ones you'll see above Tannersville.

Below Haines Falls the road is spectacular; it runs through a steep gorge with cliffs and falls and a plunging stream. At Catskill you cross the Rip Van Winkle Bridge and trade mountain grandeur for a rolling landscape of farms.

Just west of Pittsfield, Massachusetts, is the Hancock Shaker Village. Shakers were religious shunpikers (they actually practiced what they preached), and visiting this place and learning a little of Shaker values is good for anybody. Shakers lived here from 1790 to 1960 and as artisans created things of stunningly simple beauty, inspired by the conviction that an angel might have some need to use them. The Round Stone Barn here is no less a reflection of Shaker beliefs than the Sistine Chapel is a symbol of Catholic devotion.

Far, far from stormy seas, Herman Melville completed Moby Dick in Pittsfield in 1851. Since then this town along the Housatonic River has grown beyond the quaint village stage, but the common, which you will pass, is bordered by lots of big old buildings that give it a wholesome, hard-working character. Pittsfield is the largest town west of the Connecticut River, and that means you've got lots of open country in between. In that open country the Rivers and Ranges Shun meets up with the Mohawk Trail, an ancient western Massachusetts route that runs through some downright wonderful, maple-thick mountain and river scenery before spilling you into Boston.

The Mohawk Trail started out as an Indian footpath. When white people came along, they ran wagons and livestock on it. In 1789 it became our first generally recognized Shunpike; it was a free road that shunned privately owned toll, or turn), pikes. (Certainly there were other paths folks used for getting around without paying, but this was the first you could travel without fear of getting shot by the guy whose land you were on.) So revel while ye roll—the spirit of travelers' liberty lives on in every curve and gorge of the Mohawk Trail, and it flares up in billions of red and orange leaves each fall. This road is the shunpikers' equivalent of the Boston Tea Party or, better, their Declaration of Independence.

Staying Clear of Washington:

If you are taking the Rivers and Ranges Shun to or from Washington, D.C., you can leave it or pick it up in Frederick by using I-270. But what if you are just passing by and don't want to bump into your elected representative now that you've finally run him out of your home town? Can the Washington Beltway and its infamous Potomac River bridges be avoided?

Easily.

If the Shenandoah Valley fits into your plans, take US340 between Lexington, Virginia, and Frederick, Maryland. I love this road and feel a little as though I am revealing a major shunpiking secret by mentioning it. On a road map it could be misread as mountainous—that keeps turnpikers away. It actually meanders through the valley along the South Fork of the Shenandoah River between Lexington and Front Royal, Virginia, and then crosses the bulge of land that rises northward past John Brown's Harpers Ferry to Frederick. Turnpikers prefer I-81 to the west and beautiful but sometimes crowded Skyline Drive to the east. Below Front Royal the route is cupped by Massanutten Mountain and the Blue Ridge on either side. Silos pop out of the ground like monuments to the bounty of the valley; and when the season is warm and ripe the blended aroma of honeysuckle and manure is intoxicating. Here in the fall of 1864 Union troops burned the harvest to cinders, wiping out a major food source for Robert E. Lee's beleaguered army. Legend has it that crows had to pack rations to survive a valley crossing. Today, rolling along through acres and acres of crops, it is unimaginable that this land could ever have been barren.

Another alternative for bypassing Washington is to use US15 south of Frederick, which runs through some historically swank horse country in northern Virginia and links up with two good cruising roads, US17 and US29. US17 runs between Warrenton and Newport News, Virginia, and US29 parallels the Blue Ridge through the center of the state.

US17 is a lightly traveled road that is ideal for circling Washington to the west. It often has the feel of a parkway,

threading its way through tree-lined stretches as well as open farmland. There is some congestion below Yorktown; otherwise the road is about 98% gentle cruising all the way to Warrenton. Not too many miles south of Fredericksburg some folks grow acres and acres of strawberries and other U-Pick-'Em fruits and vegetables. In late June, when the sun is high and hot and the over-ripened strawberrries are begging to be picked, every passing driver becomes a sort of Ulysses, trying desperately to sail past a juicy Siren's song, in this case the syrup-thick aroma of mushed berries. You cannot resist. You will succumb. When berries are melting off the vine, you've no right to let them die. Don't fill your box too deep—you'll squash the ones on the bottom.

US29 runs along the base of the Blue Ridge eastern slope, right through the heart of Virginia. It is a wide, divided four-lane, usually without guard rails. As you travel the easy roll of this piedmont farmland you might imagine yourself in a boat cruising mammoth ocean swells, up and down smoothly. Or you can pretend this is but a small parcel of the vast lands King George granted you simply for being nice to his ugly sister. Lynchburg has a commercial strip more easily tolerated than avoided. A good time to fill up, check the oil, grease the kids with burgers and fries. The countryside north and south of Charlottesville was much loved by early presidents; Jefferson, Madison and Monroe all lived nearby. Charlottesville, grown up around Thomas Jefferson's ideal setting for the University of Virginia, would cause the man much pain were he to see it now. A shameless sprawl of shopping malls, motels and restaurants has blanketed the once-lovely pastures north of the town and bear not a hint of his love for harmony and balance in architecture.

Fortunately, you can take a pleasant shun around this strip:

Northbound: From your approach to Charlottesville on US29, take I-64 east to the exit for US250 and go west toward town. After about 1½ miles, turn right onto VA20. You are now running north, parallel to US29, only you are surrounded by pastures instead of parking lots. Turn left at US33 and then right onto US29; you are now beyond the strip.

Southbound (you are reversing the northbound directions): From US29 turn left onto US33; right onto VA20; left onto US250; right (west) onto I-64; left (south) onto US29.

Reading through this description of US29, I realize I've spent a bit of space on some unattractive features. I hope you haven't got the wrong impression. Presidents loved this land because it is beautiful and fertile. By traveling US29, you can see for yourself why they chose to settle here. Not only that, your trip is made more pleasant by easy little bypasses around Culpeper, Warrenton and, on US15, Leesburg.

Finally, I think shunpikers heading east or west through Pennsylvania should give some consideration to using US6, which connects with the Rivers and Ranges Shun just above the Cross Country Restaurant in Tunkhannock and runs along the state's northern tier. It has been years since I traveled it and I have never taken it all in one trip, but I think it is still a good road. It crosses through some of the wildest, least populated country Pennsylvania has to offer.

In a strange collision of dream and circumstance, US6 helped make a shunpiker out of Jack Kerouac, author of the Beat classic *On the Road.* Back in the '40s when Kerouac was itching to explore every possible aspect of America, he found US6 on a road map, "one long red line" that he could follow all the way across the map from Cape Cod to California. He started dreaming of all the things he'd do in all the towns he'd pass through along the way, and set out to hitchhike this one route. He didn't get very far; a torrential rain diluted his enthusiasm near the Bear Mountain Bridge over the Hudson and he gave up the turnpiker notion of taking only one road across the whole country. He decided that it was "a stupid hearthside idea. . .to follow one great red line across America instead of trying various roads and routes." This revelation in wet clothes proved fateful. From then on Kerouac left himself open to a variety of traveling choices, which led him to experiences that were "too fantastic not to tell."

If you take US6, just through Pennsylvania, you should be able to add to his story.

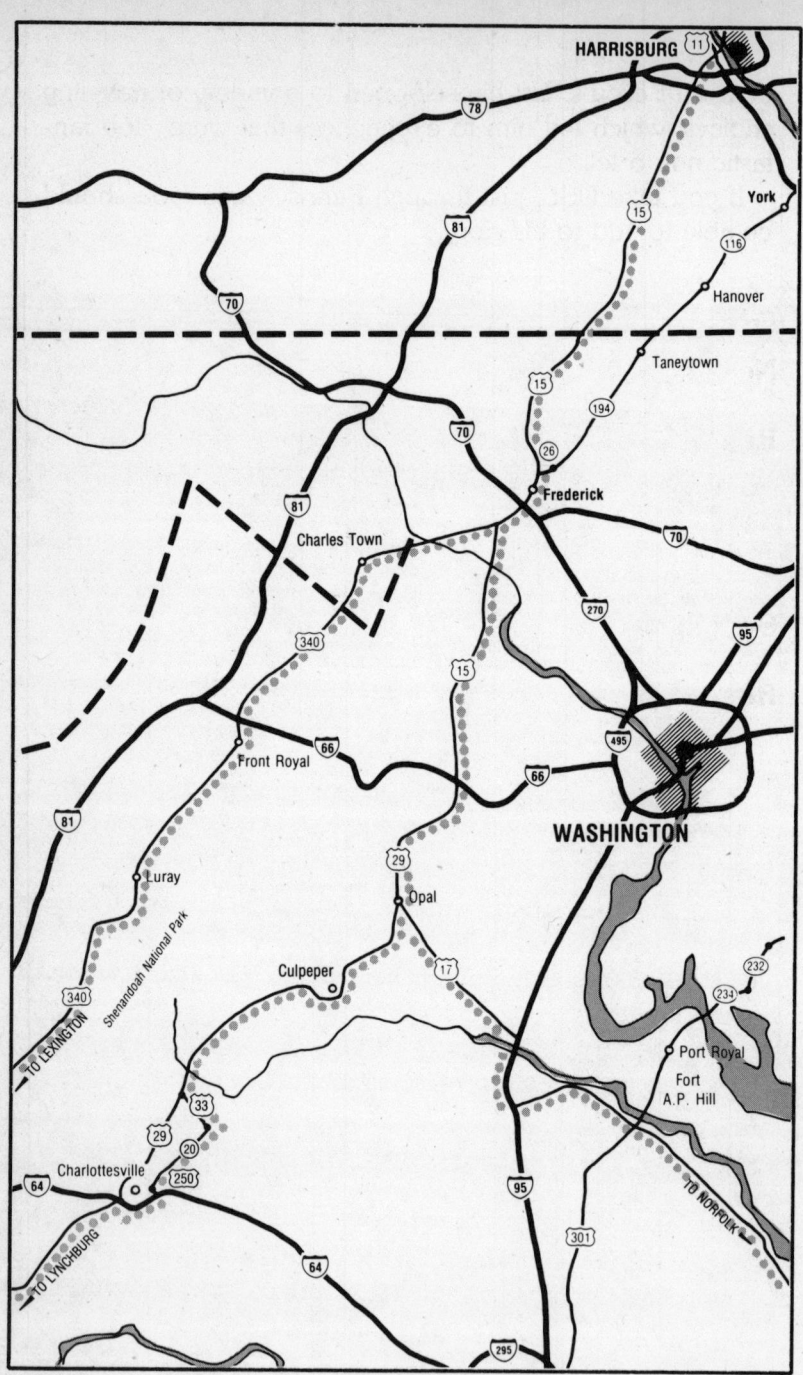

Rivers and Ranges Shun: Leg 1 and Virginia routes bypassing Washington, D.C.

Directions: Rivers and Ranges Shun
Approximately 600 miles, Washington to Boston

Leg 1
Frederick, Maryland, to Harrisburg, Pennsylvania

Northbound

Route: US15

Frederick has become quite a crossroads in recent years. Although the interchanges are pretty frantic, US15 heading north from town is well marked and you should have no trouble picking it up. The sailing is smooth all the way to Harrisburg.

Southbound

Route: US15

After turning away from Harrisburg and the Susquehanna on US15 you pass a few stoplights and then emerge into open country. Don't forget to Toad-Hop the Maryland state line.

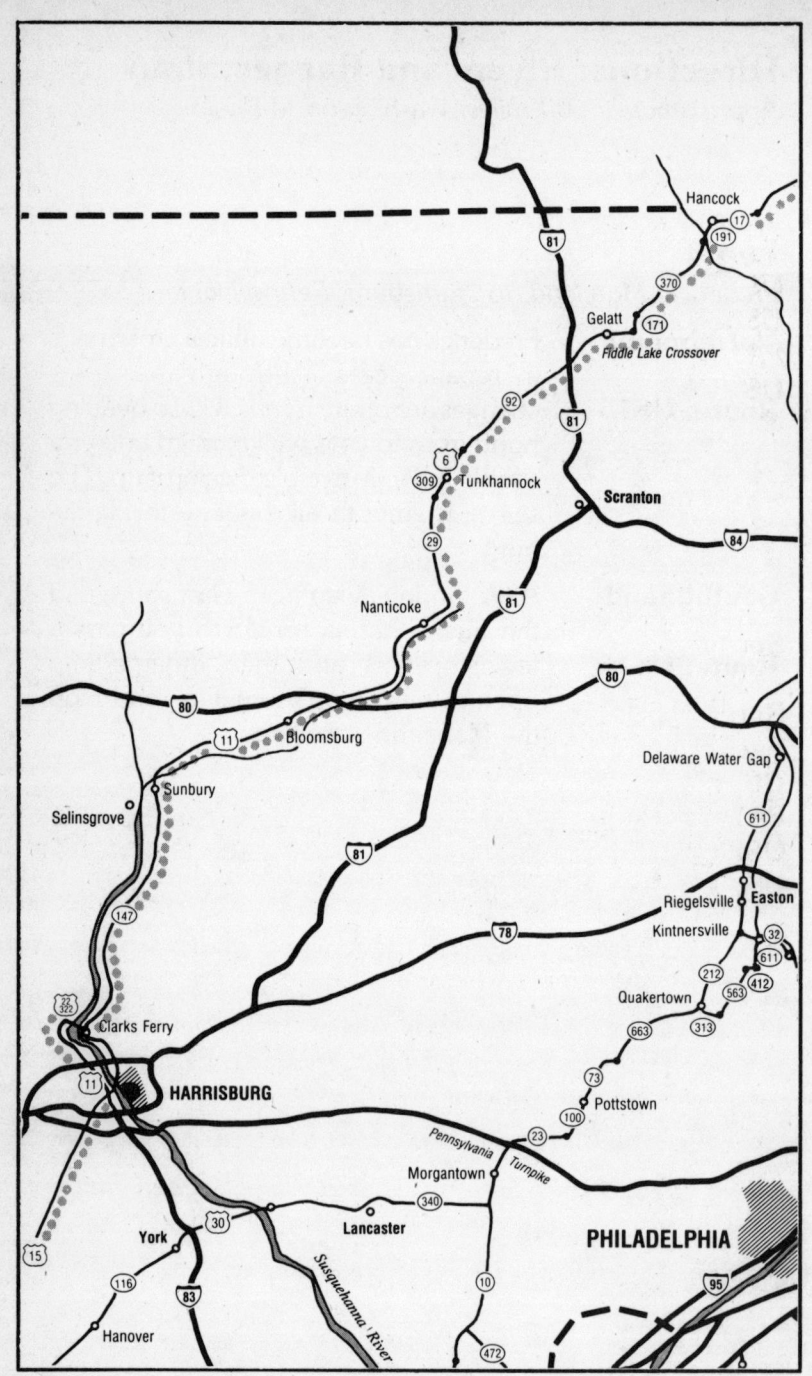

Rivers and Ranges Shun: Legs 2 and 3.

Leg 2
Harrisburg, Pennsylvania, to Nanticoke, Pennsylvania

Northbound

Route Sequence:
US11—
US22/322—
PA147—
US11

As you entered the Harrisburg area you joined up with US11. When you come face to face with the Susquehanna River and the modest skyline across it, turn left and follow US11 out of town. At the intersection of US11 and US22/322, turn east and cross the Susquehanna on the US22/322 bridge to Clarks Ferry, then follow signs for PA147 running north on the east bank of the river. Just south of Sunbury cross the new bridge that puts you back onto US11. Continue north on US11 through Bloomsburg all the way to Nanticoke.

Southbound

Route Sequence:
US11—
PA147—
US22/322—
US11

Turn right when PA29 ends at US11 in Nanticoke. Take US11 south through Bloomsburg to Northumberland. To cross the Susquehanna, wait until you cross the West Branch south of Northumberland and then use the new bridge below the confluence. Pick up PA147 and take it south to Clarks Ferry, where you use the US22/322 bridge to cross back over and rejoin US11 southbound. There is some congestion as you approach Harrisburg, but your right turn away from the river on US15 is well marked.

Leg 3
Nanticoke, Pennsylvania, to Hancock, New York

Northbound

Route Sequence:
PA29—
US6—
PA92—
Fiddle Lake Crossover—
PA171—
PA370—
PA191

As you approach West Nanticoke on US11 you will come to a stoplight. Turn left there onto PA29. (PA29 merges with PA309 about seven miles south of Tunkhannock.) At Tunkhannock turn right for a brief run on US6 east, then turn left onto PA92 and follow it until you see a sign for Village of Gelatt.

Fiddle Lake Crossover: Follow these directions; there is no numbered route. After the sign for Gelatt you will see another sign, a green one, that says "Thompson" with an arrow pointing right. Make the right, cross the stream and go through tiny Gelatt. When you come to a fork in the road bear right to Fiddle Lake. After a mile or so you will come to another fork; this time bear left. Continue past Fiddle Lake, through the few buildings that are Burnwood, then down to PA171.

Turn left onto PA171, then right onto PA370. PA370 feeds into PA191 just before you cross the bridge into Hancock, NY.

Southbound

Route Sequence:
PA191—
PA370—
PA171—
Fiddle Lake Crossover—
PA92—
US6—
PA29—
US11

Crossing the Delaware River from Hancock, NY, into Pennsylvania, take PA191 south. Within a mile you bear off to the right onto PA370. Take a left when you come to PA171.

Fiddle Lake Crossover: Shortly after you turn onto PA171 you'll see a sign pointing right for Gelatt. The road is not numbered, so use these directions. Turn right at the sign and let the road take you through Burnwood (a few scattered buildings) to Fiddle Lake. Keeping to the main road, you will gradually descend the high meadows to Gelatt. (Two forks are encountered by northbounders, but they do not come into play going south.) Cross the stream after you pass through little Gelatt and then turn left onto PA92. Take PA92 until it drops you onto US6, then continue into Tunkhannock. Turn left in Tunkhannock onto PA29/309 and stay with PA29 when it splits with PA309. PA29 takes you all the way to Nanticoke on the Susquehanna River, where you turn right and go with US11.

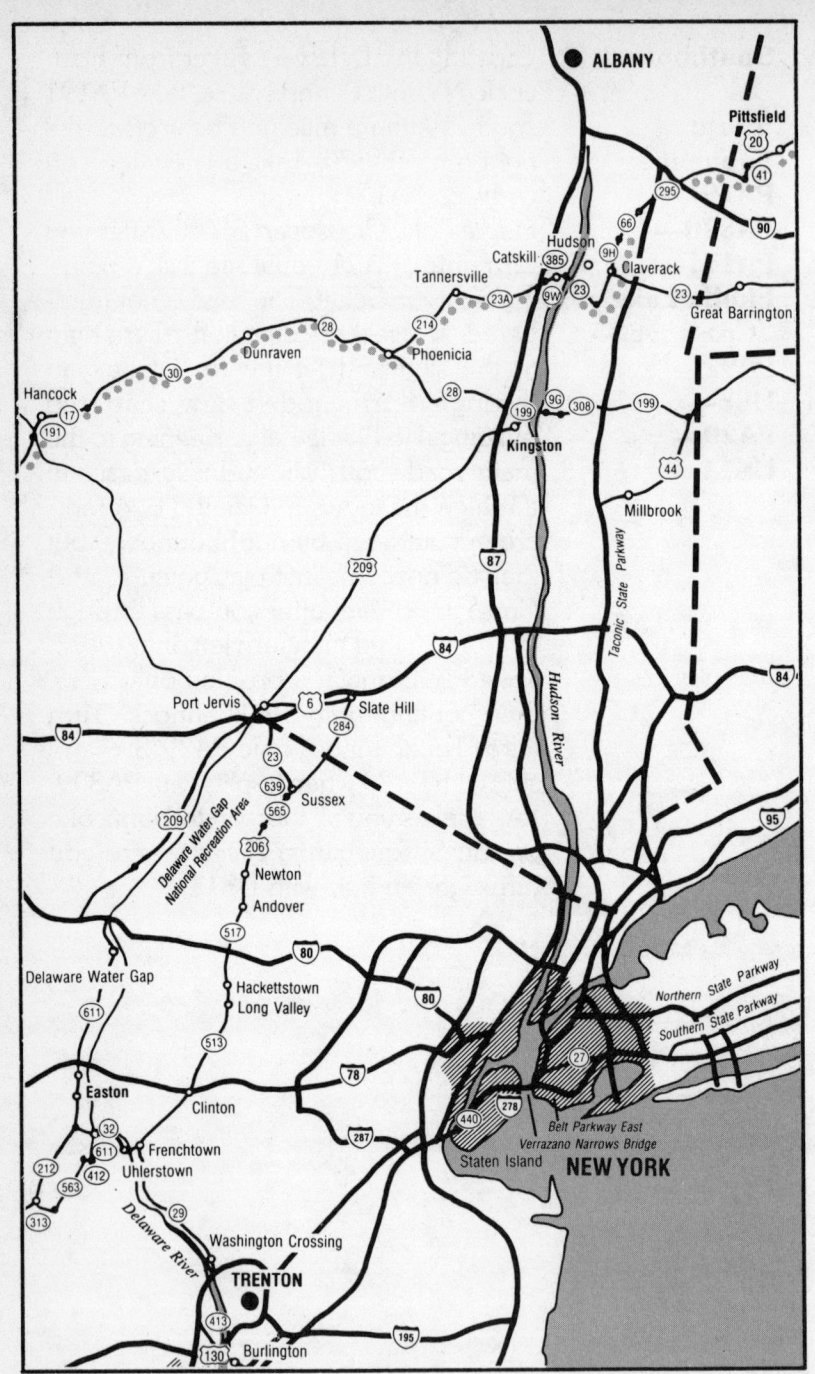

Rivers and Ranges Shun: Legs 4 and 5.

Leg 4

Hancock, New York, to Catskill, New York

Northbound

Route Sequence:
NY17—
NY30—
NY28—
NY214—
NY23A—
US9G—
NY385—
NY23

After crossing the Delaware River into Hancock, NY, make a left-hand turn and follow signs for NY17 east. Go about ten miles on NY17, then take the exit for NY30 northbound. At Dunraven turn right onto NY28 east, and at Phoenicia turn left onto NY214. As you enter Phoenicia after turning onto NY214, make an immediate left (at the Phoenicia Pharmacy) after you cross the concrete bridge. Continue on NY214 up over the pass and down, and then turn right onto NY23A just west of Tannersville. Pay attention to your driving as you wind down the fabulous gorge toward the Hudson River. NY23A feeds into US9W shortly before you come to Catskill. As you enter town, bear right onto NY385 and go straight ahead through the stoplight. Follow the signs for NY385 (making a left a few blocks after the light), then turn right when you meet up with NY23. You now cross the Rip Van Winkle Bridge over the mighty Hudson.

Southbound

Route Sequence:
NY23—
NY385—
US9W—
NY23A—
NY214—
NY28—
NY30—
NY17

As you reach the west bank of the Hudson on the Rip Van Winkle Bridge, look for a sign to the left for NY385. Go left on NY385, following the signs through town. After making a right turn you will go downhill through a stoplight at the main street then gradually uphill to US9W. Turn left onto US9W and go a short ways to NY23A, which you take west into the Catskills. Watch the road as you wind up the gorge to Tannersville; you'll be tempted to watch only scenery. On the far side of Tannersville make a left onto NY214 and go over the pass and down to Phoenicia. Follow the signs for NY214 across the concrete bridge in Phoenicia, then turn right when you come to NY28. At Dunraven go left onto NY30 and take it to the junction with NY17. Head west on NY17 to the Hancock exit, go south into town and then turn right to Toad-Hop the Delaware River into Pennsylvania.

Leg 5

Catskill, New York, to Pittsfield, Massachusetts

Northbound

Route Sequence:
NY23—
US9H—
NY66—
NY295—
MA41—
US20—
MA9

Feeling drowsy after crossing the Rip Van Winkle Bridge? Any long whiskers on your chin? Better check the date and bear left with NY23/9G when you reach the far side of the Hudson. About ¼ mile ahead, stay right with NY23 when NY9G goes left. Follow NY23 for about 4 miles to where it goes left with NY9H; make the left and stay straight on 9H when NY23 goes right at Claverack. Go right with NY66 when you come to it, about three miles north of Claverack. Bear right with NY295 when NY66 splits left and follow it into Massachusetts. Make a left turn onto MA41 and then a right turn onto US20. When you come into Pittsfield follow signs for MA9 east. (In the heart of town these signs combine with MA7 and read "7—9." You are also going "To MA8.")

Southbound

Route Sequence:
MA9—
US20—
MA41—
MA/NY295—
NY66—
NY9H—
NY23

Stay on MA9 into the center of Pittsfield; you will pick up signs for US20 west when you get to the town common. Take US20 west for four miles to a left turn onto MA41 south. Within a few miles you take MA295 west into New York. Pass under I-90 and the Taconic State Parkway, continuing with NY66 when NY295 spills into it in Chatham. About three miles northeast of the town of Hudson you go left on NY9H, picking up NY23 in Claverack. Stay with NY23 when it splits to the right from NY9H and continue on across the Rip Van Winkle Bridge into Catskill, NY.

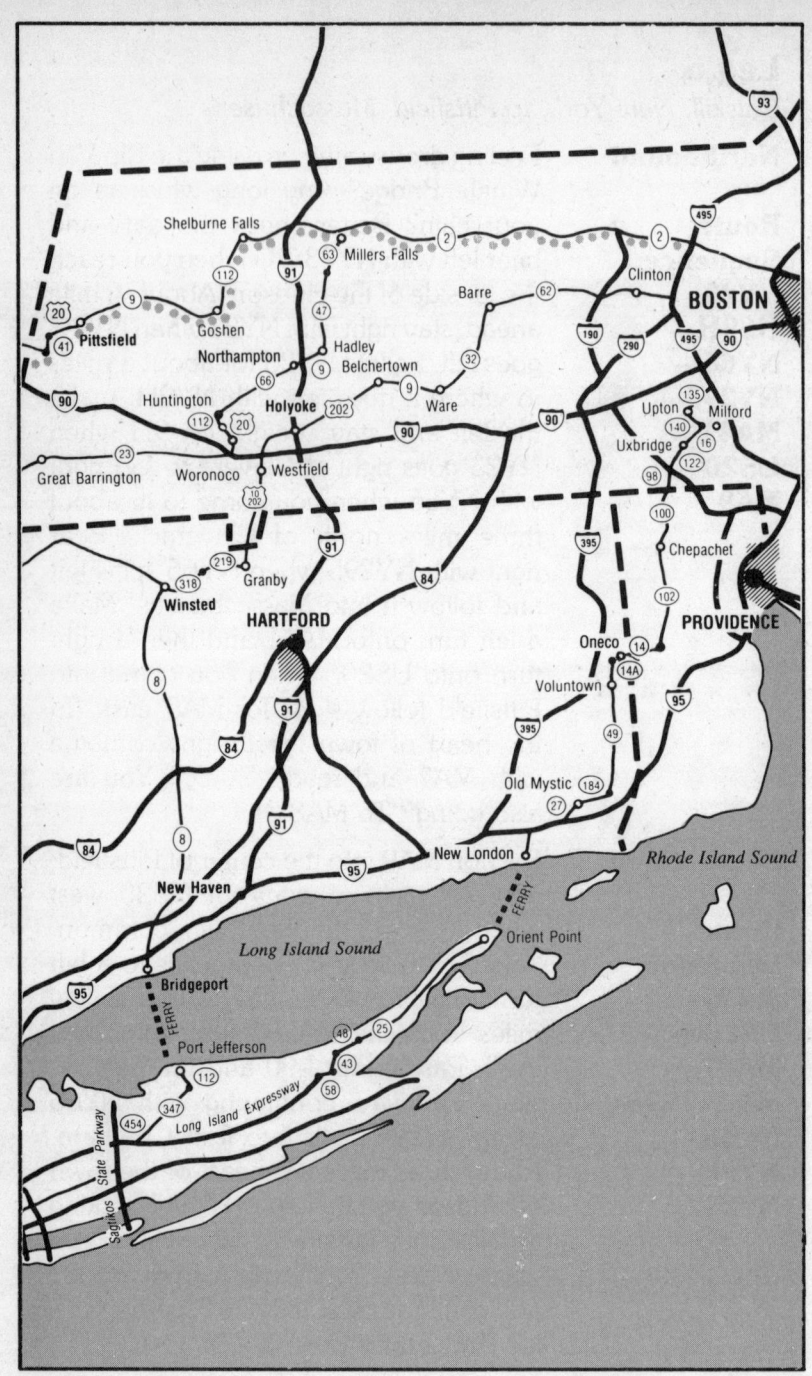

Rivers and Ranges Shun: Leg 6.

Leg 6
Pittsfield, Massachusetts, to Boston's I-495

Northbound

Route Sequence:
MA9—
MA112—
MA2

Take MA9 east to Goshen, where you make a left onto MA112 and head directly north. Get on MA2 eastbound just outside Shelburne Falls. Be careful to stay on MA2 if you want to bypass towns. Loops marked MA2A take you through the towns and are good to use if charming old main street facades are what you're after, or if you're looking for a place to gas up or eat. MA2 takes you all the way to Beantown.

Southbound

Route Sequence:
MA2—
MA112—
MA9

Cross most of the northern tier of Massachusetts by going west from Boston's I-495, past Greenfield to Shelburne Falls. Just beyond Shelburne Falls go south on MA112 and then go right (west) on MA9. Take MA9 all the way to Pittsfield and get ready to find US20 west.

The Water Gap Shun

*I shall be telling this with a sigh
Somewhere ages and ages hence:
Two roads diverged in a wood, and I —
I took the one less traveled by,
And that has made all the difference.*

ROBERT FROST
The Road Not Taken

The Delaware Water Gap, on Pennsylvania's eastern edge, is a deep river gorge that deserves a grander name. "Gap" is how we describe a hole in somebody's smile; this geographical beauty drops straight down almost a quarter mile to the Delaware River. It doesn't seem fair.

All along the Water Gap Shun you will encounter odd names, the variety of which certainly confirms that you could only be in America. You don't have to go to England to see Nottingham, Oxford and Cambridge; they're all within a few miles of each other in southeastern Pennsylvania. Dublin is just a little ways south in Maryland. Maybe a Pennsylvania pioneer took his bearings in Compass, and then tasted sweet water in Honey Brook. Are there any churches in Churchville, Maryland? Quakers still living in Quakertown, Pennsylvania? French Huguenots in Huguenot, New York? Surfers in Monterey, Massachusetts?

I think the Dutch are responsible for all the killing in Pennsylvania and New York. Like Bushkill and Basherkill, and of course Catskill. (There's a Murder Kill in Delaware; it supposedly means Mother Creek, but who's brave enough

to ask?) Indians contributed Shawnee, Shawangunk, Wawarsing, and Pataukunk. But what's the story behind Neversink, Accord and Kripplebush? And Cuddebackville?

From Baltimore the Water Gap Shun runs northward, skirting the congestion of Amish country tourist traps and curling through mostly farmland between the substantial Philadelphia sprawl and Allentown-Bethlehem. It follows the Delaware River upstream through the Gap all the way to New York, where it picks up the course of the Neversink River and Basherkill, at the base of Shawangunk Mountain's long ridges. Then it's over the Hudson at Kingston, along the Taconic Parkway and due east through the heart of the Berkshires. Crossing the Connecticut River at Northhampton, Massachusetts, it heads north along the river through some superb pastoral scenery before joining the Mohawk Trail and MA2 eastbound into Boston.

The Water Gap Shun takes off from the Baltimore Beltway (I-695) on MD7, known long, long ago as the Old Post Road or Philadelphia Road. It is something of a marvel. Sandwiched between hectic I-95 and commercial US40, two very heavily traveled highways, it glides up and down gentle hills for about 15 miles, through woods and pastures and over streams, with no sign of its neighbors' traffic. Hula Doll loved the bop and roll of it. It has been so since 1666, when this was the main thoroughfare through the wilderness to Philadelphia. Somehow over the centuries, Maryland highway builders never flattened, gorged or straightened the Old Post Road, never pulled it taut like a rope on a gallows. There is only a little congestion as you depart the Beltway past a shopping mall, then it's loose and comfortable down on the farm. Enjoy it.

Some of the lushest farm country found anywhere in the East cushions your route through southeastern Pennsylvania. You may see some Amish carriages, but you will be east of the major Amish tour spots in Lancaster County. The "simple folk" are very heady capitalists and have managed to translate their heralded plain lifestyle into huge crowds of shoppers, the worst of it between PA10 and Lancaster on US30. If you want to get a closer look without getting caught up in the commercial hubbub, roam the backroads just north of PA340 toward Intercourse. (See also Variation 1.)

The route begins to parallel the Delaware River just south of Easton. It also runs alongside the old Delaware Canal, which is now a very long state park running from Easton to Bristol, northeast of Philadelphia. If a picnic is in your plans, keep an eye out for the Canal Museum on the river side of the road before you get into Easton. It is situated at the confluence of the Lehigh and Delaware rivers and their respective canals, and it borders lots of open ground and paths by the water. Pennsylvania once had more than a thousand miles of canals, and a century and a half ago this place was hopping. Millions of tons of Pennsylvania coal were barged down the Lehigh Valley to Easton and then down the Delaware Canal to Philadelphia for shipping. The museum is small but gives a good picture of canal days and their folklore, just the kind of museum you can handle when traveling.

The US209 portion of the Water Gap Shun between East Stroudsburg, Pennsylvania, and Port Jervis, New York, is often the first timid venture away from turnpiking made by would-be shunpikers in the Northeast. Stampeding along on I-80 eastbound, for example, turnpikers can look at their road atlas and see that US209 runs north to I-84. It's not too far, their thinking goes. Looks pretty safe. Even if there are lions and tigers and bears, oh my, in this brief stretch of unknown, the turnpikers can lunge for the I-84 lifeline before being devoured. This isn't exactly the spirit of Lewis and Clark reborn, but at least they're trying. However, most of them can't cope with the sudden absence of trucks (commercial traffic is prohibited) and the fact that this road allows them to pull off just about anywhere they like. Most of them return to the comfort of interstate predictability, which is good for everybody. We can't have cattle roaming all over the countryside. Besides, they're happier behind the fences. A select few, though, can't believe their good fortune. Should have tried this sooner, they sometimes say. By the time they've reached I-84 the road atlas has been replaced

by a neglected New York state road map, dug out from under the seat among the candy wrappers and beer cans. They continue north, past I-84, on US209, but who knows where they'll go next? The woild is their erster, they sometimes say. Little baby shunpikers they are, and the landscape says hello there, come on in.

The actual Delaware Water Gap is below Stroudsburg, at a sharp bend in the river. You can't miss it; the valley walls plunge steeply and the word gap starts to make sense. The river has spent a few million (billion?) years cutting this gorge 1,200 feet down through the rugged mountain terrain, and zowwee! what an impressive piece of work. Add some fall reds and oranges to the thick forests pouring over the edge and, with a little squinting, it looks like molten lava cascading to the river below.

For a couple of miles on the south end of the Delaware Water Gap National Recreation Area you might think you made a wrong turn somewhere. Don't worry. The Poconopalace motels aren't allowed inside the park. Suddenly that stuff will vanish, leaving you with forests, deer, ponds, waterfalls and, of course, the river. Dingmans Falls, a short walk through the woods above the visitor center, is another diversion good for a picnic. Until the late 1960s the falls and the surrounding land were privately owned and operated as a tourist attraction. Miles of gaudy billboards made sure travelers couldn't miss the turnoff for wondrous Dingmans Falls. Some things need to be offered to the public in a very low-key manner, and natural attractions are certainly among them. My first visit to the falls was after the billboards had disappeared, about 20 years after I had first passed up the opportunity. They are not so special as a sideshow fat lady, maybe, but the setting is very beautiful and the water comes tumbling down with a mighty roar.

There is a ghoulish story linked to the town of Milford, Pennsylvania, at what is now the north entrance to the

National Recreation Area. The Delaware Valley used to be the domain of the Iroquois, Delaware, Shawnee and Lenni-Lenape Indian tribes. You may not have heard of the Lenni-Lenape; after having lived in the area for about 5,000 years, they were almost totally wiped out within 100 years of their first contact with Europeans. In the mid 18th century a desperate band of the once-thriving Lenni-Lenape raided and killed whites along the Delaware River in the hills of western New Jersey. Among the victims was Thomas Quick of Milford. Quick's son, Tom Jr., promised to avenge his father's death by killing 100 Indians. For the next 40 years, until his death of smallpox, Tom Quick murdered Indians whenever the chance arose. But he fell short of his goal, managing to shoot, stab and otherwise take the lives of only 93. According to the story, Tom kept up the killing long after his death, and more successfully than before. In their own act of vengeance Indians unearthed Quick's body, chopped it up and sent pieces to Indians far and wide, thereby spreading the lethal smallpox among themselves.

Arnold Gingrich, founding editor of *Esquire* magazine, once wrote a book called *The Well-Tempered Angler*. It is something of a classic, I have been told (I think that means it didn't sell very well), and a fishing friend of mine, who studies the mental and spiritual aspects of coaxing gilled creatures into his hands simply to set them free, encouraged me to read it a while ago. He actually lent me his personal copy. I was instructed to finger the pages with clean hands only, and to genuflect at every mention of the word "trout."

Gingrich wrote at some length about fishing the Neversink River, which begins high in the Catskills and drains down to join the Basherkill along US209 and empty into the Delaware at Port Jervis, New York. Recalling that the author had discussed this oddly named stream (incidentally, I think the name is derived from a Lenni-Lenape word), I referred back to the book hoping to find some choice descriptive quotes on the region that I might pass on to you. Well, I am quite sure that Mr. Gingrich fished the Neversink—there is

ample evidence to support that—but I am much less certain that he ever *looked* at it. There isn't a single statement about the Neversink geography. If not his whole body, his whole mind spent the entire time under water, in various pools where wily Neversink trout (down on one knee, please) might be found. As far as that goes, it seems the submarine view was splendid, even when he got skunked, which seems to have been often. He returned many times, had a little routine mapped out in fact, whereby his weekend began on Esopus Creek high in the Catskills and ended along the Neversink after following a remote mountain track down from the mountains. And nary a word about the rugged beauty that surrounded his descent. So it must be with such fervent fishers of fish, whose heads are always submerged.

I can tell you this: Shawangunk Mountain, a favorite of rock climbers, rises boldly like a huge wall on the east side of the route, above the Neversink and Basher Kill, which accompany you for about 40 miles. Although I have never found it so, there are probably times when the road is busy, Sunday evenings perhaps, but the nearby Interstates suck up most of the area traffic. That leaves you to enjoy the apple orchards, farms, small towns and, of course, the Neversink.

MA23 through the Berkshire Hills runs moderately up and down, allowing good pace (Hula Doll's favorite kind of road to dance down). Thick with trees and streams, it is also a good place for birding. I camped one night in early spring just south of Otis, along a lively brook banked with trees as well as some open ground. My fire built and supper dishes done, I sat back to watch the lingering evening fade. It was not to be. A catbird landed on the picnic table and then flew back to a nearby tree. He did this several times, giving his nasal cat-call each time he went back to his perch. In another tree, a warbler that I could not positively identify launched into a terrific twilight serenade, several clear, strong, refreshing notes repeated in pattern for almost 20 minutes, or so it seemed. A pair of vireos flitted through the branches, busy, busy, busy in their last search for food before dark. Above the woods a hawk circled against the sky.

As if all this activity wasn't enough, just as most good little birds were settling in for the night a woodcock came careening madly through the near-darkness and landed in the grass only a few yards from Stan the Van. He stood there motionless for a time and then took off again, his wings beating out the weird whistling sound that identifies this nocturnal species. Several times he landed near me, seeming to invite my approach, but just as I moved too close he was up and off again, his whistle very close and then very far a few times over until he landed once again. I couldn't make any sense out of his flight pattern; it was pell-mell up and down stream and then around in circles. He kept it up well beyond nightfall.

Rounding out my evening with the birds, I managed to get the Orioles game on the radio. They flapped their wings mightily, which produced another weird whistling sound, sort of like a bomb diving to earth.

Northampton was the home of quiet Calvin Coolidge, who once remarked, "If you don't say anything, you won't be called on to repeat it." It was also the springboard for the first great religious revival in America. Jonathan Edwards, a brilliant young preacher who would have found nothing useful in Silent Cal's advice, came to town in 1729 intent on saving the souls of wealthy Connecticut River merchants. And how. Flames of hellfire consumed the congregation when he preached, so much so that one rich man with a guilty conscience slit his own throat rather than live with the prospect of spending eternity in the devil's domain. Edwards's emotional oratory was an instant hit with sinners of every stripe: "O sinner! Consider the fearful danger you are in: 'tis a great furnace of wrath, a wide and bottomless pit, full of the fire of wrath, that you are held over in the hand of that God. . .you hang by a slender thread, with the flames of divine wrath flashing about it, and ready every moment to singe it, and burn it asunder." He even used

the phrase "fire and brimstone," and made eternal damnation sound just awful: "How dismal will it be when you are under those racking torments to know assuredly that you never, never shall be delivered from them. . .and when you shall have worn out the age of the sun, moon and stars in your dolorous groans and lamentations. . .yet you shall have no hope, but shall know that you are not one whit nearer the end of your torments." (Sounds like a typical back-up at the Delaware Memorial Bridge.)

Edwards wanted his flock to open their hearts and let God bring them a redeeming experience. Northampton, and soon the rest of Massachusetts, ate it up. Parishioners moaned their "dolorous groans" as the preacher's accusing finger pointed their way; they wept and shouted and lamented the sinful state of their souls. Some got right down on the floor and let it all hang out, writhing in torment.

For about 20 years, a good time was had by all.

You will notice a distinct change in the landscape as you follow the Connecticut River north of Northampton. This valley is the most fertile ground in all New England. Once the bottom of a vast glacial lake, it caught all the silt washed down from the north. There are no outcroppings of rock here, just flat, open country dotted with trees, farm buildings and a few towns.

If you want to ogle at America's future in training at Amherst College, and travel a portion of US202 walled in by forest, stay on MA9 eastbound. When you get to the Amherst town common, which is a rectangle, go left and then right, exiting the common diagonally from where you entered. That'll put you on the road going to Quabbin Reservoir and old US202 north to MA2.

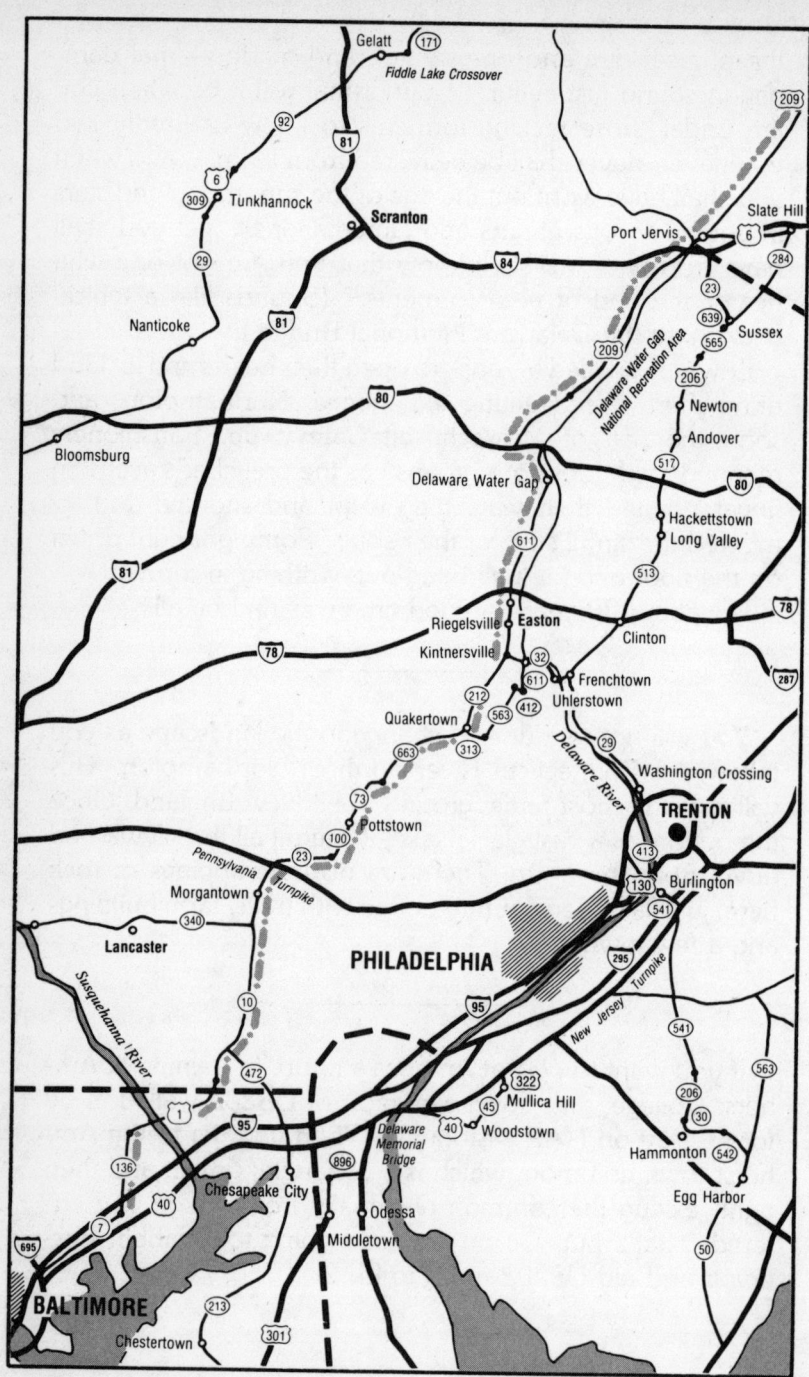

Water Gap Shun: Legs 1 and 2.

Directions: Water Gap Shun

Approximately 475 miles, Baltimore to Boston

Leg 1
Baltimore Beltway to Pottstown, Pennsylvania

Northbound

Route Sequence:
MD7—
MD136—
US1—
PA10—
PA23—
PA100

From the Baltimore Beltway (I-695) take Exit 34, the first exit east of I-95, and go north on MD7. After about 15 miles turn left onto MD136, go another 15 miles to a right turn at US1 heading north. Cross the Susquehanna River, pass into Pennsylvania and go north on PA10 as far as Morgantown. Turn right onto PA23, blow a kiss to the masses as you cross the Pennsylvania Turnpike, and then get on PA100 running north to Pottstown. There is a nice Hungarian deli with great sandwiches on PA100 just south of the intersection with PA23.

Southbound

Route Sequence:
PA100—
PA23—
PA10—
US1—
MD136—
MD7

Once on PA100, go past Pottstown to PA23, where you head west to Morgantown. Boo and hiss at the penned-in mob on the Pennsylvania Turnpike, then turn south on PA10. Ride PA10 south all the way to US1, taking in some of America's finest farm scenery along the route. Take US1 south into Maryland, cross the Susquehanna, then turn left onto MD136. MD136 spills into MD7, which takes you all the way to the Baltimore Beltway (I-695) one exit east of I-95.

Leg 2

Pottstown, Pennsylvania, to Port Jervis, New York

Northbound

Route Sequence:
PA100—
PA73—
PA663—
PA313—
PA212—
PA611—
I-80—
US209

About six miles north of Pottstown you exit PA100 and go east on PA73 to a left turn on PA663. In Quakertown PA663 becomes PA313; take it down the tree-lined streets into the old business part of town. You will see a complicated-looking fork in the road. Don't panic. Turn left and look for signs for a left onto PA212. PA212 takes you north, and also eases you down into the Delaware River valley where you meet PA611. Turn left and follow PA611 through Easton (just follow the signs; they're clearer than any directions I could give you) to Delaware Water Gap (a town at the actual Gap). There you get on I-80 west for one exit, then go north on US209 through the Delaware Water Gap National Recreation Area to Port Jervis, NY.

Southbound

Route Sequence:
US209—
I-80—
PA611—
PA212—
PA663—
PA73—
PA100

Continue on US209 across the Delaware River to Milford, PA. Just south of Milford you enter the Delaware Water Gap National Recreation Area. Go through the park; on the south end pick up I-80 eastbound. Take the first exit you come to; the sign says Delaware Water Gap and PA611. Go south on PA611 through Easton (well marked) to PA212 just below Riegelsville. Turn right and follow PA212 through Quakertown. (In the old business part of town there is a poorly marked fork in the road; just stay right and continue straight ahead.) At a busy traffic light on the edge of town PA212/313 ends, becoming PA663.

Take PA663 down through Pennsburg to PA73, where you turn right. Go through Gilbertville on PA73 and then turn left onto PA100 south.

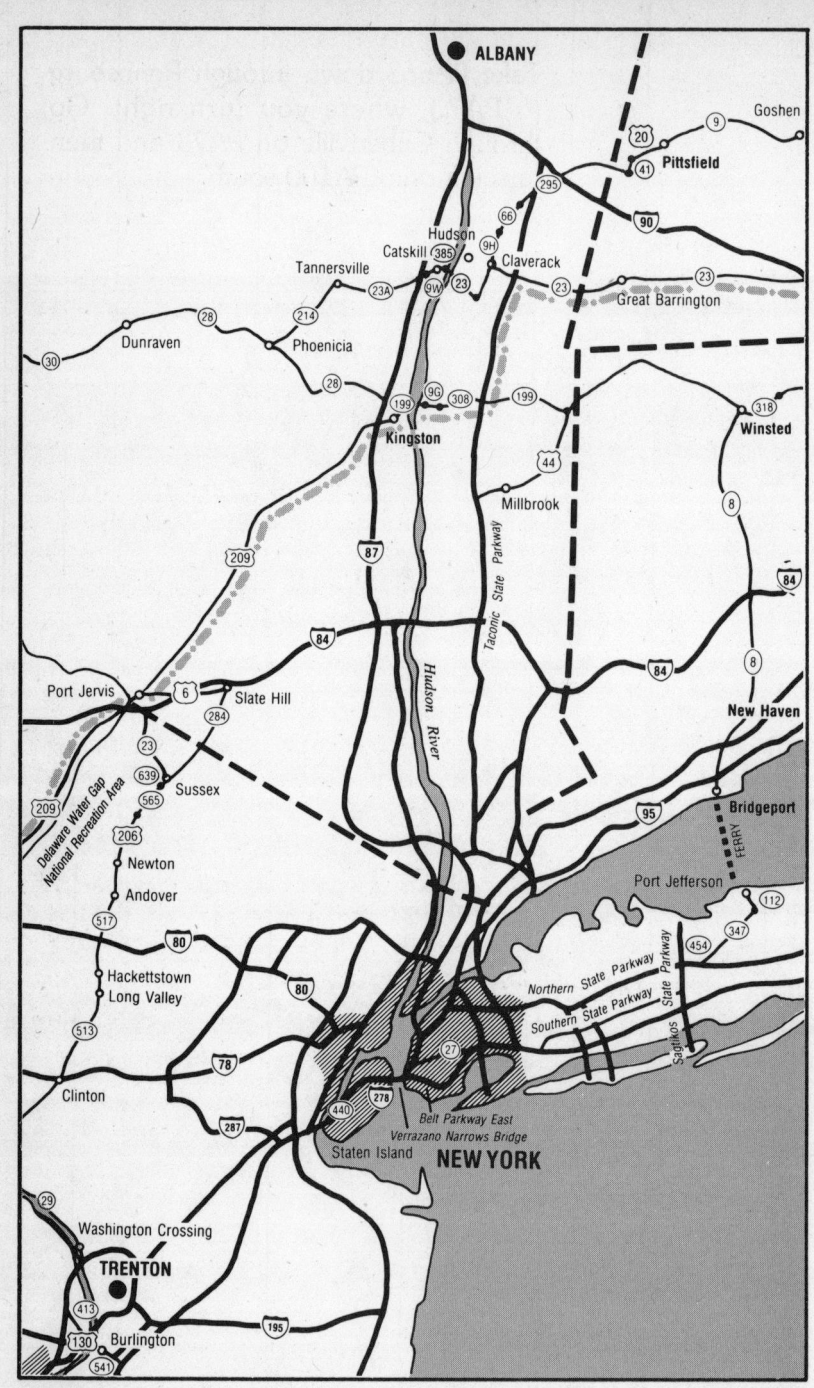

Water Gap Shun: Leg 3.

Leg 3
Port Jervis, New York, to Great Barrington, Massachusetts

Northbound

Route Sequence:
US209—
NY199—
NY9G—
NY308—
NY199—
Taconic State Parkway—
NY/MA23

Follow US209 through Port Jervis, then all the way up to Kingston, on the Hudson. When US209 becomes a divided freeway follow signs for the Kingston Bridge. Cross the Hudson and pick up NY199 eastbound. In about a mile you will come to NY9G; turn right and head south another mile or so to NY308, which you take to the east. You will shortly pick up NY199 again; it will take you to the Taconic State Parkway. Go north on the Parkway to NY/MA23 eastbound and follow it to Great Barrington, MA. (Don't forget to Toad-Hop the state line.)

Southbound

Route Sequence:
MA/NY23—
Taconic State Parkway—
NY199—
NY308—
NY9G—
NY199—
US209

Continue west on MA23 to New York and the Taconic State Parkway. Go south on the Parkway to NY199 and head west, making a left onto NY308 and then a right onto NY9G northbound. (You are following signs for the Kingston Bridge.) Cross the mighty Hudson and pick up signs for US209, which you ride all the way down through Port Jervis into Pennsylvania and the Delaware Water Gap National Recreation Area.

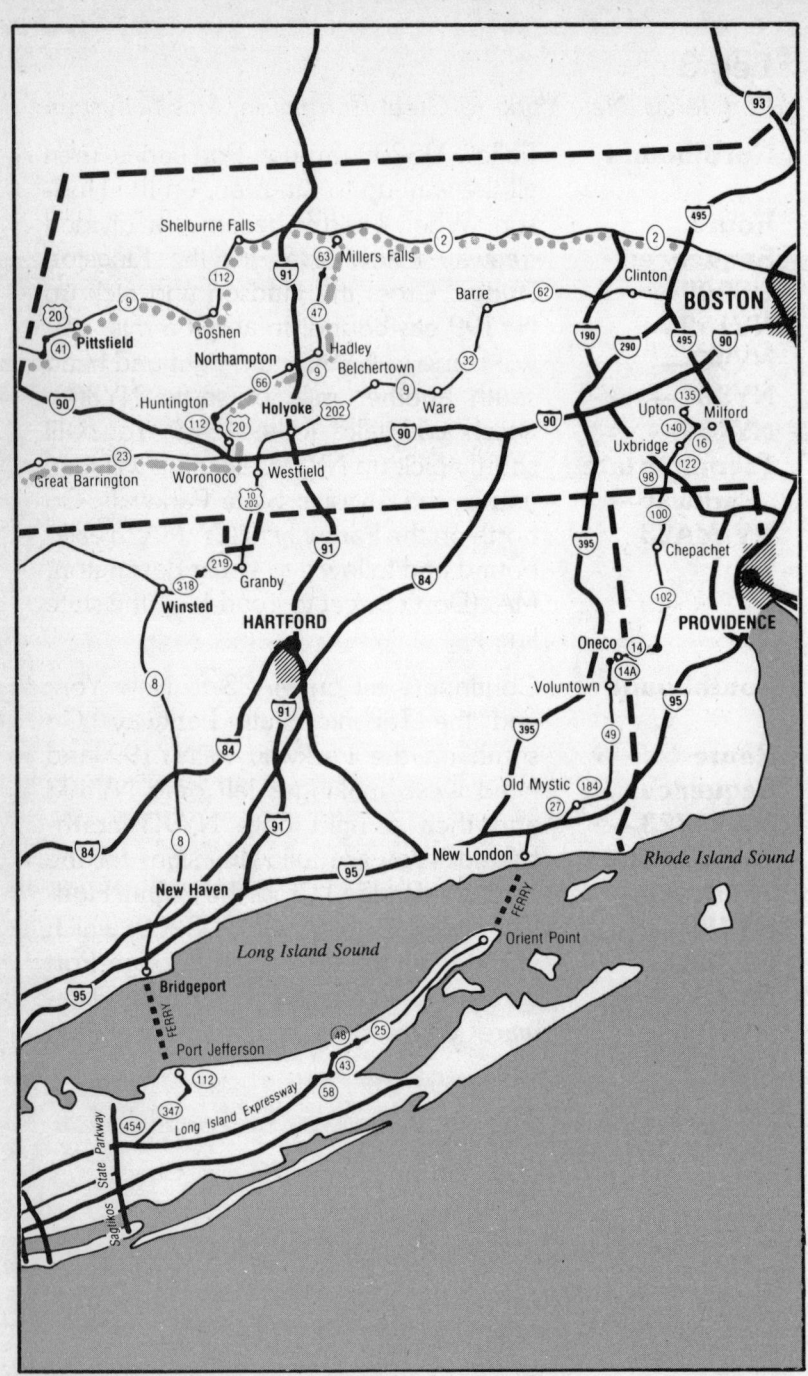

Water Gap Shun: Leg 4.

Leg 4
Great Barrington, Massachusetts, to Boston's I-495

Northbound

Route Sequence:
MA23—
US20—
MA112—
MA66—
MA9—
MA47—
MA63—
MA2

Stay on MA23 through Great Barrington and the Berkshire Hills to the junction with US20 in Woronoco. Make a left onto US20. Go to Huntington and take MA112 to the right off US20. Turn right onto MA66 after about four miles. In Northampton look for signs for MA9 eastbound and take it across the Connecticut River. At Hadley turn north (left) on MA47, which spills you onto MA63 northbound. Follow signs for MA2 eastbound when you come to Millers Falls and then cruise on MA2 all the way to Boston.

Southbound

Route Sequence:
MA2—
MA63—
MA47—
MA9—
MA66—
MA112—
US20—
MA23

From Boston's I-495 take MA2 west. Just before you reach the Connecticut River turn south on MA63, and then turn right onto MA47. When MA47 meets MA9 go west, crossing the Connecticut River into Northhampton. There you pick up MA66 westbound. Go to MA112, turn left and go to US20. Make a right onto MA23* and take it through the Berkshires to Great Barrington.

*At Otis, ferrypikers can take MA/CT8 directly south to the Bridgeport Ferry.

The Ferrypike

What a beautiful journey! The air is balmy, the wind is gentle. There is the ocean, the big blue ocean.

JEAN DE BRUNHOFF
The Travels of Babar

You get on a boat and what do you do? You start waving. You wave at people on shore and you wave at people on other boats. You don't know any of them, but you just feel like waving. If you see the skipper up on the bridge you wave at him too. You can't help it.

There is something so beautiful about setting sail that people are always given to waving. It seems no matter the voyage, be it a paddleboat ride on a pond or a transatlantic crossing on a giant liner, people are always lifting an arm in gentle souls' greetings to one another, a soft pink palm offered instead of a mean ol' fist. People really want to like each other and waving proves it.

Ferrypiking will help you be more likeable. I know this because it happened to me.

Due to an unfortunate incident, I wasn't ready to like anybody before I took a ferry ride across Long Island Sound. Yet I wound up a pretty charming guy, telling long stories with little bits of truth in them to an equally charming fellow who told me wonderful tales about old trains and railroading. We had chosen spots next to each other along the small ferry's rail. We got splashed occasionally and that made us smile the way people do when they've been dunked but don't mind a bit. He was coming back early from his vacation because it was his turn to be engineer on a train the next day. He belonged to a club of some kind that was devoted

to preserving a small stretch of old track and a locomotive and some cars. On weekends he and his club friends took folks for rides back and forth on the track. The friends rotated jobs; engineer, conductor, coalman and so on. He loved old trains and I loved how he talked about them. This guy even loved shoveling coal. There was something in him that was enviably simple and steady, and forthright like steam power. Had he been born 50 or a hundred years earlier he'd have made a terrific railroad man, a big and fleshy coalman with soot on his face, or a friendly tickets-please conductor with a watch fob looped across his vest. But he was not, and trains were just his hobby.

As I say, I was not too likeable—surly probably describes it best—when I took my place on the rail. I had just had a run-in with an off-duty cop in Middletown, Connecticut, who had appropriated a crowded street for his own use. He had threatened me with "I'm a cop in this town," so I'd better not get in his expletive-expletive way or I'd get my tender Virginia expletive deleted. I wonder what he says on traffic safety day at the elementary school. The worst part was his physique, a trim version of socialist sculpture. I don't think he's much of a waver. I had to back down to avoid having my teeth scattered all over the expletive road.

Well, no sooner had the ferry left the dock than I forgot about Middletown's finest. The sun glittered all over everything. Kids ran up and down the decks looking for the secret places ships always seem to have. Sailboats scooted by, and at the stern gliding seagulls dipped down to accept french fries from a little girl's hand. She held out her offering to a flock of about 50 birds, not one of which had to beat a wing to keep up with the boat. A couple in their 60s had come aboard on a motorcycle and sidecar. They were just touring around for fun, and there was something reassuring about seeing members of an older generation dressed in denim and leather. I don't even remember how the conversation with the train buff got started. I wound up having a blast on a day that had begun pretty poorly, and landed at the tip of Long Island refreshed and ready to wave at anybody, even a cop.

This ferrypike takes you through the cornfields of eastern Maryland and Delaware; across the mouth of the Delaware Bay to Cape May, New Jersey; into the wilds of the Jersey Pine Barrens and to ancient Batsto Village; across the Verrazano Narrows Bridge and out onto Long Island, either to the ferry that runs between old Port Jefferson and Bridgeport, Connecticut; or further to the ferry between Orient Point and New London, Connecticut. (Until some enterprising genius launches a ferry service between the Jersey coast and Long Island, the middle leg of this shunpike runs with turnpikers from North Jersey out a ways onto Long Island. It makes setting sail all the more delicious.) From Bridgeport the Ferrypike runs directly north from the urban coast to the Berkshires in western Massachusetts. From New London it quickly finds some classic New England scenery in eastern Connecticut and Rhode Island before coming to the outskirts of Boston.

I've come to the conclusion that there is hardly a bad road to be found on the flat peninsula that includes Delaware and eastern Maryland and Virginia. This area is known variously as the Delmarva, or Mardelva, Peninsula, and the Eastern Shore. It has also been called the Land of Pleasant Living. As long as you steer clear of summertime beach traffic, the driving is pleasant too. If one road doesn't suit you, try another.

At Lewes, Delaware, the ferry landing and resaurant/gift shop are built on the site of an old unknown sailors' boneyard. Over a period of 400 years, whenever the surf handed back to shore a seaman who had been lost at sea, nearby residents put him here with others who had met the same fate. Grim testimony to the hardships of life during the heyday of sail. Almost 200 years ago my Exton ancestors left England and sailed safely past this spot after nine weeks at sea. They landed in Philadelphia to begin their new life in the New World.

Across the mouth of the Delaware Bay is schizophrenic Cape May, New Jersey, an old resort town that can't decide what its personality should be. Part of it is chintzy modern motels that look as if psychedelic Timothy Leary had supervised the painting and lattice crews. The architecture

supports descriptions like cinder block Victorian, and the purple incest of quaint. Away from the beach strip, however, is the other Cape May: the old cottages, homes, churches and other buildings that retain a dignified turn-of-the-century charm. If you want to break your Ferrypike into two comfortable days, lodging in *old* Cape May is a very nice way to do it.

It might surprise you that there is lots more to New Jersey than industry, gambling and the turnpike. Most of your shunpiking on this route is through an area known as the Pine Barrens, a nearly impenetrable wilderness of pitch pine forest in a sandy soil. Here and there enterprising farmers have cleared away the forest to establish blueberry farms, and if you pass by in late June or July, signs will invite you to pick your own.

Deep within the Pine Barrens, about five miles west of NJ563 along NJ542, is Batsto Village. Beautifully restored by the state, Batsto grew up around an ironworks that produced cannon and other munitions for the American Revolution and the War of 1812. Competition from richer iron ore sources in Pennsylvania eventually eclipsed Batsto and turned it into a ghost town. Nowadays the ironmaster's house and other buildings are open to visitors, the old mill cuts wood solely by water power, and Connie Birdsall, the adorable postmistress, hand-stamps your postcards on request and delivers a great big smile for no charge.

I have been unable to find a satisfactory shunpike around the turnpiker-riddled underbelly of New York—specifically the Jersey Amboys, Staten Island and Brooklyn—and I do apologize. I once asked a veteran of these roads when the Friday afternoon traffic dies down. His reply: "Sunday night." It's not quite that bad, but the point is well made: try to hit this stretch sometime other than rush hour.

When I was a little boy, I sat in the church pew on Sundays and thought reverently about cleansing the black splotches of sin from my soul, which I imagined was located under the flesh and bone blade of my left shoulder. I wondered too where sins went once they'd been washed away, and became concerned that an eventual bounty of washed-off sins might one day endanger the natural environment.

Now that I have seen the Great Dump on Staten Island, I no longer wonder where sins go, nor do I worry about sin pollution. I'm convinced it all goes to this dump, and as long as it can be contained here we'll all be safe. Ordinarily I wouldn't wax eloquent about sending shunpikers past a pile of garbage (it runs along NY440), but this one is something to behold. It's so high you can't get over it, so wide you can't get around it, and so foul it must be sinful. This, folks, is the clogged drain to hell.

As you get out a ways onto Long Island the urban sprawl gradually ends, and disappears completely if you are going out to Orient Point. It's downright rural out there. Farms and vineyards dominate the landscape. Port Jefferson, with its narrow streets and fashionable storefronts, is a pleasant place to stroll around if you have time. Watch your wallet—prices are steep.

There isn't anything particularly attractive about Bridgeport or New London, other than meeting or debarking the ferries. The shunpike out of Bridgeport follows the Connecticut River north; the farther you go, the lovelier it gets. Above Waterbury to the Massachusetts state line and the Berkshires the population thins and the forest thickens. From New London north toward Boston you cross lots of brooks worth fishing and pass lots of farms cut out of the woods, their boundaries drawn with stone walls.

Here are some nuts and bolts for planning your ferrypike:

Cape May/Lewes Ferry
P.O. Box 827
North Cape May, NJ 08204

Information:
  Cape May Terminal: 609-886-2718
  Lewes Terminal: 302-645-6313
  (Delaware State Travel Service will send you schedule and rates; call toll free 800-441-8846)

Big ferries. Longer than a football field, wide enough to carry six rows of cars and trucks. There is plenty of deck space to stroll or find your special place in the sun. Kids love to explore. Seven days a week, all year long, ferries make the 75-minute trip between Lewes, DE, and Cape May, NJ. Departures are usually hourly during the summer, a little less often during spring and fall, and four times daily in winter. Summer departures begin at 7 A.M. from Lewes, 8:40 A.M. from Cape May. If lounging under a dolphin-blue sky isn't appealing, you can check out the fast food, game arcade or gift shop. Restrooms and a water fountain, too.

Bridgeport & Port Jefferson Steamboat Company
102 W. Broadway
Port Jefferson, Long Island, NY 11777

Information and reservations:
  Port Jefferson Terminal: 516-473-0286 (recording)
                           516-473-0631 (office)
  Bridgeport Terminal: 203-367-3043 (recording)
                           203-334-5993 (office)

In service during summer only. From Port Jefferson ferries depart about every hour and 45 minutes beginning at 7 A.M.; same intervals from Bridgeport beginning at 8:45 A.M. These are slightly smaller than the Cape May/Lewes ferries, but they have a double-decker arrangement that accommodates almost as many cars. The crossing of Long Island Sound is supposed to take 90 minutes but can be just over an hour on calm days. Flat water kills the fun though. These boats have a full bar (now, now...remember you're driving), fast food. Alas, no video games.

Cross Sound Ferry Service, Inc.
Box 33
New London, CT 06320

Information and reservations:
  New London: 203-443-5281
  Orient Point: 516-323-2743

Runs all year, and has increased crossings around holidays, including Thanksgiving and Christmas. During the peak summer season ferries leave both terminals at 7 A.M. and run hourly until 9 P.M. from New London, 10 P.M. from Orient Point. Sailing time is given as an hour and a half. The fleet is a hodge-podge of big and little boats, and you never know what you're riding until you board. The largest can carry 100 cars, the smallest about 20. (I prefer the little one. The breeze seems cooler somehow, and your chances are better for getting sprayed.) All have food and restrooms.

    Advance reservations can be made for all these ferries, but that means you've got to be very organized in your travel plans and arrive for the one ferry you pick. And that's a great way to ruin your shunpiking state of mind. Presumably you are taking the ferry so you can relax. Such planning is likely to make you feel rushed; and rushing is a turnpiker trait. (For what it's worth, I have never made a reservation and I've always made the next ferry.) However, the Great Spirit Hula Doll has made one concession to this world of schedules: she says it's OK to make a reservation if you're traveling on holiday and height-of-summer weekends, when lots of people want to ride the ferries. But if you dash around and make a general turnpiker's ass out of yourself just to catch the ferry, your shunpiker's license will be revoked.

The Cape May/Lewes Ferry is the least expensive; the Bridgeport & Port Jefferson the most. A family of four can make a crossing for about $22 to $32. You've had more expensive impulses. We certainly have: My wife and I once bought a $100 boom box, one of those huge portable radio/tape players that kids strut around with at full blast. The sole purpose for buying this thing was so we could listen to Ella Fitzgerald sing Cole Porter while we camped in the wilderness of a national park. We thought it would fit in with the surroundings; sort of like having practically perfect music in a practically perfect natural environment. We were wrong. We never thought we'd feel uncomfortable listening to "Begin the Beguine," "April in Paris," "It's Delovely" and all the rest. We did. We had split a practically perfect silence, and felt ashamed. We turned the damn thing off. It now sits quietly on top of a book case, a complete waste of money.

You'll never say that about taking the ferry.

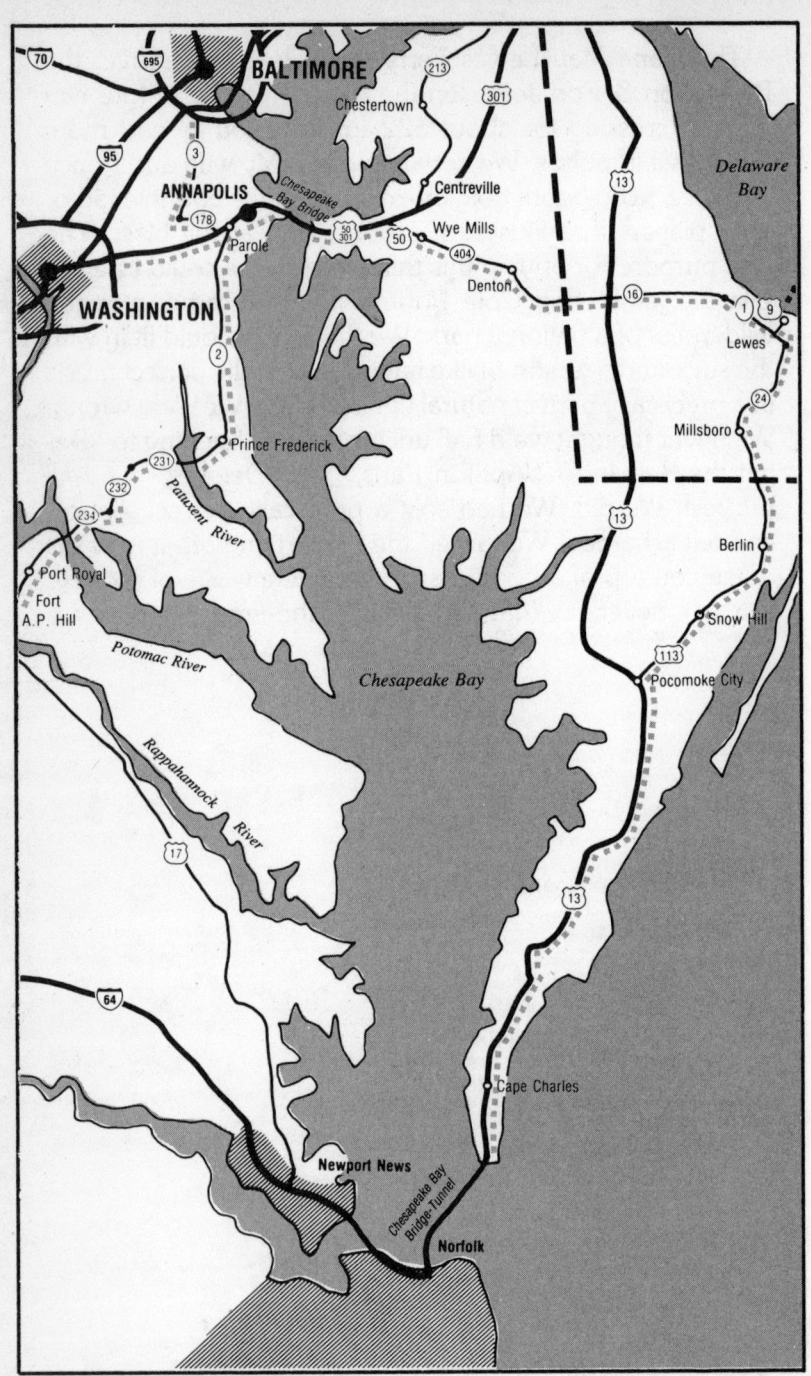

Ferrypike: Legs 1, 1-N and 2.

Directions: Ferrypike
Approximately 500 miles, Washington to Boston

Key to Plotting the Course of Your Ferrypike
(Southbounders remember to read *backwards*)

If you are ferrypiking between:	This is your Leg sequence:
Baltimore/Washington/Richmond and Boston	1—2—3—4—5-OP—6-NL (assumes you take Orient Point Ferry from Long Island to New London, CT)
Baltimore/Washington/Richmond and western Connecticut/Massachusetts	1—2—3—4—5-PJ—6-B (Port Jefferson Ferry from Long Island to Bridgeport, CT)
Norfolk and Boston	1-N—3—4—5-OP—6-NL (Orient Point—New London Ferry)
Norfolk and western Connecticut/Massachusetts	1-N—3—4—5-PJ—6-B (Port Jefferson—Bridgeport Ferry)

Leg 1*

Baltimore/Washington/Richmond to Chesapeake Bay Bridge

North- and Southbound

Begin/End Baltimore: Between Baltimore's I-695 and Bay Bridge use MD3—MD178—US50. MD2 looks better on the map, but it is heavily developed between Glen Burnie and Annapolis.

Begin/End Washington: Use US50.

Begin/End Richmond: Use Leg 1, Jersey Surprise Shun.

Leg 1-N

Norfolk, Virginia, to Cape May/Lewes Ferry

Northbound

Route Sequence:
US13—
US113—
DE24—
DE1—
US9
(go to Leg 3)

Cross the Chesapeake Bay Bridge—Tunnel from Norfolk to Cape Charles on US13 and continue north into Maryland. At Pocomoke City bear right with US113, following it past Snow Hill and Berlin into Delaware. Go right with DE24 at Millsboro, then left onto DE1 just south of Lewes. Bear right onto US9 following signs for the ferry and Cape Henlopen State Park.

---

*Be careful not to confuse the Chesapeake Bay Bridge, near Annapolis, with the Chesapeake Bay Bridge-Tunnel, at Norfolk.

Southbound

Route Sequence:
(from Leg 3)
US9—
DE1—
DE24—
US113—
US13

Turn right out of the ferry parking lot and take US9 out of Lewes. Go left at DE1, then make a right onto DE24 after about one mile. Head south on US113 in Millsboro, staying on it until you merge with US13 in Pocomoke City, MD. US13 takes you the entire length of Cape Charles and across the Chesapeake Bay Bridge—Tunnel into Norfolk.

Leg 2
Chesapeake Bay Bridge to Cape May/Lewes Ferry.

Northbound

Route Sequence:
US50—
MD404—
MD/DE16—
DE1—
US9

Off the Bay Bridge stay with US50 at the fork with US301 and continue to Wye Mills, where you go left onto MD404. About five miles after Denton make a left onto MD16, which quickly becomes DE16. Turn right onto DE1. When you come to the congestion outside Lewes, be on the lookout for a left turn onto US9 to the ferry and Cape Henlopen Sate Park. This comes *after* the turn for Business US9.

Southbound

Route Sequence:
US9—
DE1—
DE16—
MD404—
US50

Make a right turn out of the ferry parking lot and follow US9 to DE1. Go right on DE1 and then left on DE16, which takes you all the way to Maryland. Turn right onto MD404 and follow it to another right onto US50 west. US50 takes you across the Bay Bridge.

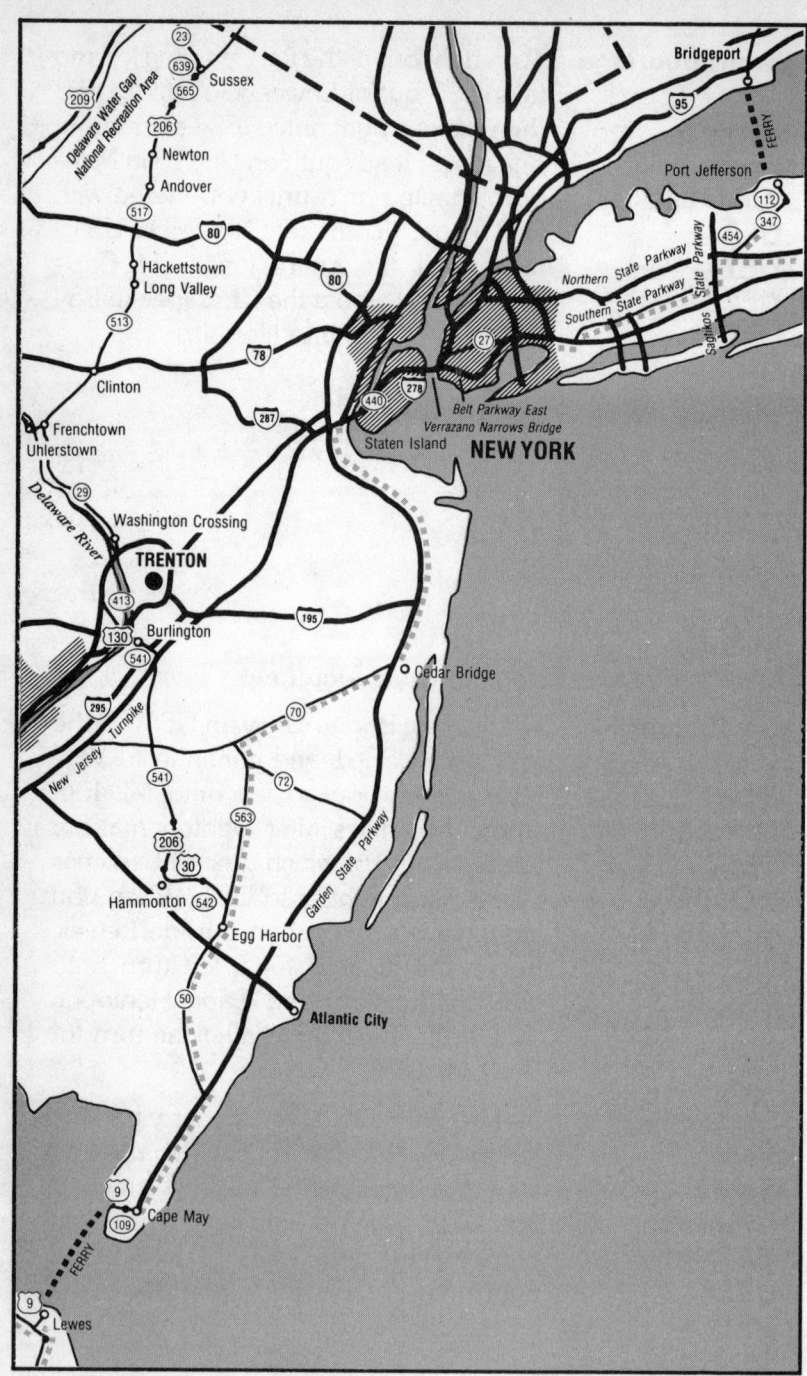

Ferrypike: Legs 3 and 4.

Leg 3
Cape May, New Jersey, to Cedar Bridge, New Jersey (jct. Garden State Parkway)

Northbound

Route Sequence:
US9—
NJ109—
Garden State Parkway—
NJ50—
NJ563—
NJ72—
NJ70

When you pull off the ferry in New Jersey, start looking for signs for the Garden State Parkway. You will travel short distances on US9 and NJ109 before you reach the Parkway, which you take north to Exit 20S. There you pick up NJ50 northbound to Egg Harbor, where it becomes NJ563. Stay on NJ563 (you can pause to pick blueberries) through Wharton State Forest to NJ72. Turn left on NJ72, then go right off the traffic circle on NJ70 eastbound, all the way to Cedar Bridge where you again ride the Garden State Parkway.

Southbound

Route Sequence:
NJ70—
NJ72—
NJ563—
NJ50—
Garden State Parkway—
NJ109—
US9
(Norfolk-bound go next to Leg 1-N)

Exit the Garden State Parkway at Cedar Bridge (Exit 88N) onto NJ70 westbound. Go through Lakehurst to Lebanon State Forest. When you come to the circle junction go almost all the way around before heading southeast on NJ72. Four miles down NJ72 turn right onto NJ563, which takes you through Wharton State Forest and a zillion acres of blueberries. At Egg Harbor pick up NJ50 and take it all the way to your entrance onto the Garden State Parkway. At the southern end of the Parkway follow signs for the Cape May/Lewes Ferry. You will briefly travel NJ109 to US9 south to the ferry.

Leg 4

Cedar Bridge, New Jersey, to Sagtikos State Parkway, Long Island

Northbound

Route Sequence:
Garden State Parkway—
NJ/NY440—
I-278—
Belt Pkwy—
NY27—
Southern St. Parkway—
Sagtikos St. Parkway

Go north on the Garden State Parkway to NJ440, where you go east to Staten Island and your road becomes NY440. Enjoy the dump while you can, because you have to leave it when you go east on I-278 to the Verrazano Narrows Bridge. As you come off the bridge take the left exit for Belt Parkway East/Kennedy Airport. Once on the Parkway follow the signs (little airplanes) for Kennedy Airport. Near the airport you merge briefly with NY27 and pick up signs for Southern State Parkway. Don't take Sunrise Highway (NY27). Follow Southern State Parkway east to Sagtikos State Parkway and go north. Now you must decide which ferry you'll take.

Southbound

Route Sequence:
Sagtikos St. Parkway—
Southern St. Parkway—
NY27—
Belt Pkwy—
I-278—
NY440—
Garden State Parkway

Go south on the Sagtikos State Parkway and then take the Southern State Parkway west. Follow signs for Kennedy Airport; you will merge with NY27 and pass the airport. When NY27 veers right you go left on the Belt Parkway to the Verrazano Narrows Bridge. Once you are on the bridge you are heading west on I-278. Go south on NY440, marvel at the Great Dump and what it means, and then take the Outerbridge Crossing into New Jersey. Head south on the Garden State Parkway to the junction with NJ70.

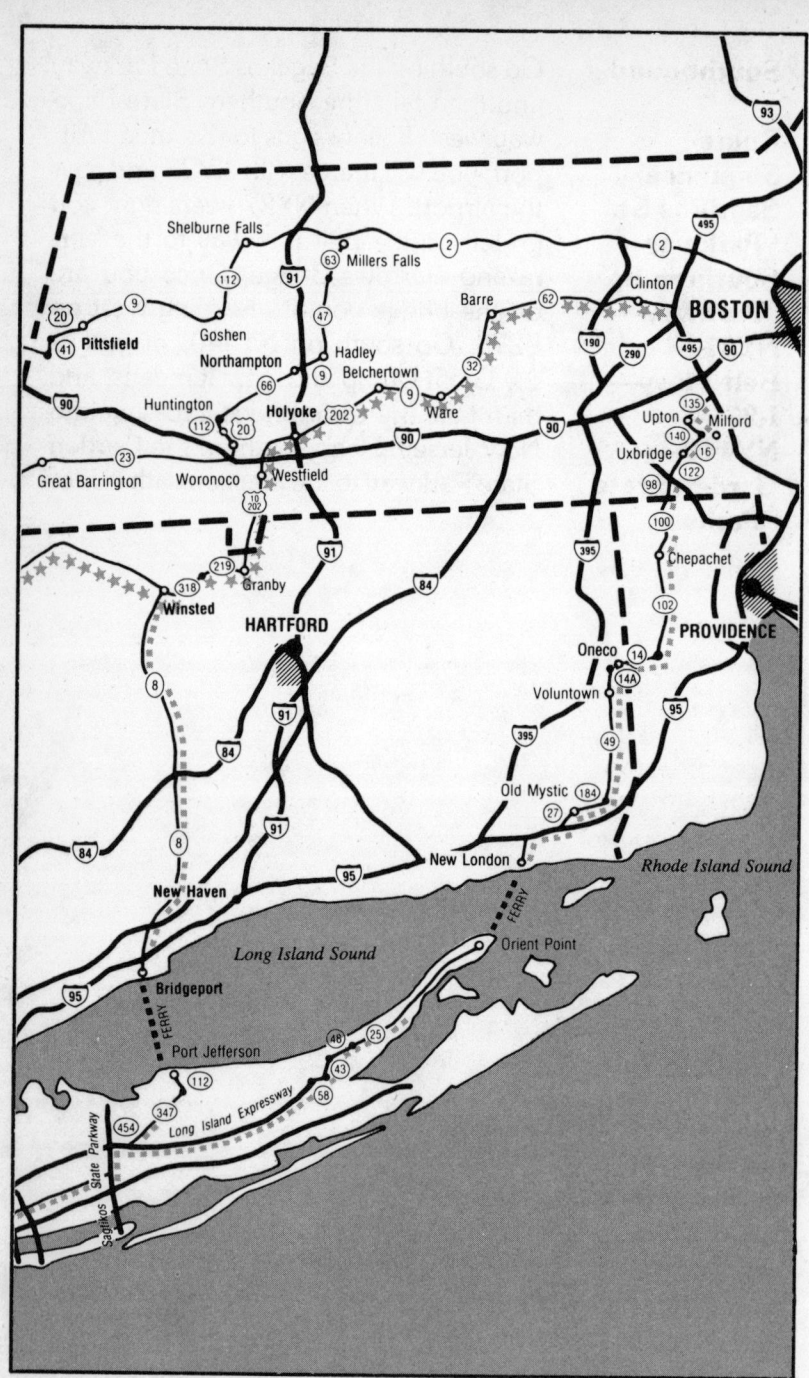

Ferrypike: Legs 5-PJ, 5-OP, 6-B and 6-NL.

Leg 5-PJ
Sagtikos State Parkway to Port Jefferson Ferry

Northbound

Route Sequence:
Northern St. Parkway—
NY454/Veterans Hwy—
NY347/Nesconset Hwy—
NY112

From the Sagtikos State Parkway go east on the Northern State Parkway until it drops you onto NY454 (Veterans Highway) east-bound. Pick up NY347 (Nesconset Highway) and take it east to NY112. Go north on NY112 until it deadends at the ferry dock in Port Jefferson.

Southbound

Route Sequence:
NY112—
NY347/Nesconset Hwy—
NY454/Veterans Hwy—
Northern St. Parkway—
Sagtikos St. Parkway

NY112 heads directly away (south) from the Port Jefferson ferry dock and takes you to NY347 (Nesconset Highway). Go west on NY347 and merge with NY454 (Veterans Highway). Veterans Highway takes you west to the Northern State Parkway. Go to the first exit on the Northern State Parkway and take the Sagtikos State Parkway south.

Leg 5-OP
Sagtikos State Parkway to Orient Point Ferry

Northbound

Route Sequence:
NY495 (L.I. Expressway)—
NY58—
NY43 (Northville Tnpk)—
Sound Ave—
NY48—
NY25

From the Sagtikos State Parkway take NY495 (Long Island Expressway) to its eastern end. Continue east on NY58 to a traffic circle, then go to the third traffic light and turn left. You are on NY43 (Northville Turnpike). Cross NY105 and turn right at Sound Avenue. This becomes NY48 and then NY25. Follow NY25 to the end of the line, which is the Orient Point ferry landing.

Southbound

Route Sequence:
NY25—
Truck 25/ West 48—
NY43 (Northville Tnpk)—
NY58—
NY495 (L.I. Expressway)

After debarking at Orient Point, follow NY25 for about eight miles and then bear right with Truck 25/West 48. Stay on West 48 as far as NY43 (Northville Turnpike), where you make a left. Cross NY105 on NY43 and then go right onto NY58. Get on NY495 (Long Island Expressway) and take it in to the Sagtikos State Parkway, which you want to take south.

Leg 6-B
Bridgeport (CT) Ferry to Winsted, Connecticut (joins Jersey Surprise Shun, Leg 5)

Northbound

Route: CT8

To get to CT8 from the Bridgeport Ferry dock, go right out of the dock area onto Water Street and then make a left onto State Street where a multilevel parking garage stands on the far left corner. Make another left onto Lafayette Street and then a right onto Prospect. Your ramp to CT8 (and CT25) goes off to the right. (You can prepare for this by getting the ferry schedule while on board and checking out its Bridgeport map.) Once on CT8 just ride it north to Winsted, where you can pick up Leg 5 of the Jersey Surprise Shun or continue north to Leg 4 of the Water Gap Shun.

Southbound

Route: CT8

From Winsted drive directly south to Bridgeport on CT8. The ferry company gives these directions for getting to the dock: "From Routes 25 and 8: Take Exit 1 (Myrtle Avenue), stay straight to third light. Go left at light. Stay straight to ferry."

Leg 6-NL
New London (CT) Ferry to Boston's I-495

Northbound

Route Sequence:
I-95—
CT27—
CT184—
CT49—
CT14A—
RI14—
RI102—
RI100—
RI/MA98—
MA122—
MA16—
MA140—
MA135—
I-495

Out of the ferry parking area take a right onto Water Street and continue straight to the ramp for I-95 north. Go to Exit 90 and take CT27 north to Old Mystic. Take CT184 east; when you come to the rotary (traffic circle) stay on CT184 by following signs for Providence and Food. Rotary Pizza-Grinders has the food. At the blinking light turn left onto CT49 to Voluntown. Continue north through Voluntown, where you follow signs to Oneco, still on CT49. Turn right when CT49 ends at CT14A, go through Oneco, merge with CT14 and cross into Rhode Island (RI14). A stop sign indicates the junction with RI102; turn left. At Chepachet turn left with signs for Woonsocket-Putnam and pick up signs for RI100 to Harrisville. Within a mile signs point you right onto RI98; follow it (Toad-Hopping into Massachusetts) until it ends just under the MA146 overpass. Turn left and then go with the sign that says Bear Right to Uxbridge. You will spill into MA122, which goes into Uxbridge. Turn right onto MA16. On the western outskirts of Milford turn left onto MA140 north to Upton. In Upton you will come to the Wood Pharmacy on your left and a Texaco station on your right; turn right there with the signs To Rte. 135 and Hopkinton 6 Miles. You will intersect with I-495 in about five miles.

Southbound

Route Sequence:
I-495—
Upton road—
MA140—
MA16—
MA122—
MA146—
MA/RI98—
RI100—
RI102—
RI/CT14—
CT14A—
CT49—
CT184—
CT27—
I-95

Take Exit 21 off I-495 for West Main Street and Upton. At the crossroads by the lake continue with the double yellow lines; when you come to a stop and face a white church turn left onto MA140 south. There is a sign. The intersection with MA16 is clearly marked. You go right with MA16 west to Mendon, and then to Uxbridge where you make a left onto MA122. Bear right with the sign for MA146 south; just past the ramp for new MA146 turn right onto MA98 (opposite a night spot currently called Thee Inferno). Follow this road into Rhode Island—it becomes RI98—until it ends at RI100. Go left and pick up signs for RI102 south. Continue straight with RI102 at a blinking yellow light just beyond the state police office. Not quite 15 miles south on RI102 make a right onto RI14. Just as you enter Connecticut bear left onto CT14A, go through Oneco and turn left onto CT49 south. Follow signs for CT49 through Voluntown and continue south to CT184. Go west on CT184, keeping straight through the rotary, to CT27 at Old Mystic. Turn left on CT27 and get on I-95 southbound. Take Exit 84 South for Downtown New London, turn left at the second light onto Governor Winthrop Boulevard. When it ends turn left and then right into the ferry parking area.

——— **Variations** ———

I travel not to go anywhere.... I travel for travel's sake.

ROBERT LOUIS STEVENSON

Hark! What's this? A new squiggle on the map? Come spouse! Come kids! I must drag thee down yet another road to adventure, discovery, and yes, eventually your grandmother!

If you are a shunpiker in good standing, you won't follow the shunpikes I have outlined here exactly, at least not after your first trip on one. You'll begin to itch for variety. Who knows what wonders a little voluntary detouring might uncover?

When I was turning down just about any road I pleased in doing my research for this book, I sometimes came upon things I'd never dreamed of seeing (which for me is the whole point). Such as the rusty skeleton of a ferris wheel in central New Jersey. Who has ever imagined the death of a ferris wheel? In the middle of an overgrown lot, it was sticking up in the sky all alone as if the carnival had suddenly abandoned it here one night many years ago. What could they say in the next town when they showed up without the ferris wheel? The whole community had been looking forward to a ride on it. Yet somebody left it behind, exposed to the wind and rain and winter ice. A cold, merciless killing.

Needless to say, the picture of that forlorn, rotting ferris wheel has stuck in my mind. I have fun with the thought of it. I think about poor Mr. Merry-go-round trying to sound so cheerful after losing his old friend Mr. Ferris. Mr. Calliope, who didn't see any point in sticking around, eloped with the sexy little Cotton Candy machine, who would stick to

anybody. The Bumper Cars jumped the fence and went scurrying off into the woods. Free at last, they played tag down the backroads and hide-and-seek in the bushes. Even now, when you wander down a quiet country road, you can sometimes hear them giggling silly little beep giggles, just beyond where you can see.

One other thing about the ferris wheel. Most of the seats had been pried off and carted away. Somebody is probably watching a made-for-TV movie on one right now. Or maybe it's in the rumpus room so kids can sit in it, put the bar down, and play ferris wheel.

Here are a few suggestions to get you started shuffling up your shunpiking.
(Directions for southbound travelers are the exact reverse of northbound directions unless otherwise noted.)

Variation 1: Rivers and Ranges Shun (Leg 1) connects with Water Gap Shun (Leg 1) by way of US15—MD26—MD194—PA116—US30—PA340—PA10 in southeastern Pennsylvania.

From US15 just north of Frederick, Maryland, exit right onto MD26 and then left onto MD194 north to Hanover, Pennsylvania. At Hanover pick up PA116 to York and US30 east. Just east of Lancaster take PA340 east to PA10 and go left.

There is sometimes a slow light where PA116 meets US30, and congestion on the bypass around York; otherwise the route between Frederick and York is delightful, passing the birthplace of Francis Scott Key near Taneytown, Maryland, and covering beautiful horse country on wide open, lightly traveled roads. Southbounders approaching York on US30 are met with a sign confessing the number of lights you must endure (I think it's eight, most of them synchronized). I like the honesty. On the east bank of the Susquehanna in Columbia is the Watch & Clock Museum, a spectacular little place full of some of mankind's most ingenious devices for measuring time, many of them ticking

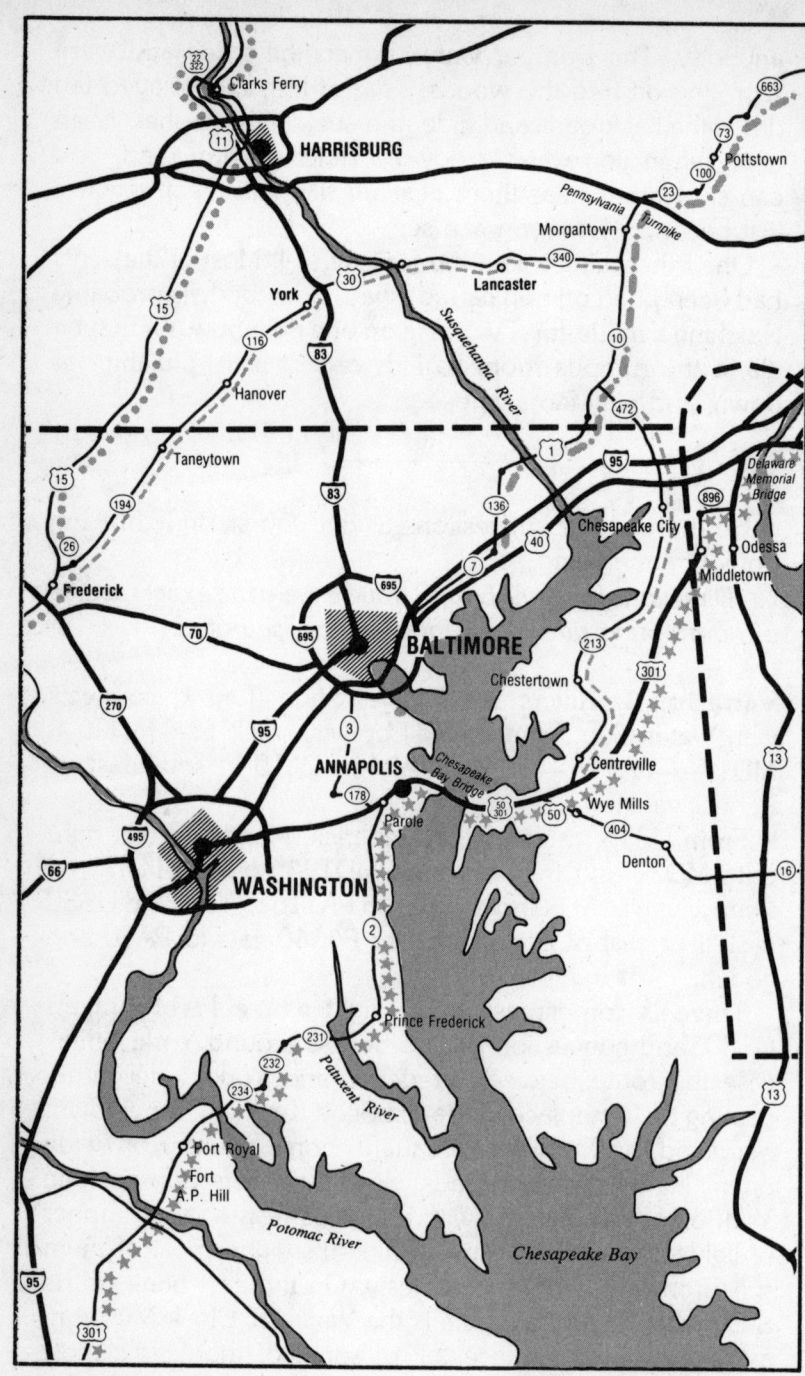

Variations 1 and 2.

away merrily. Be there on the hour for all the chiming and cuckoos. Follow the signs from US30. East of Lancaster is Amish country, and PA340 goes through some of the best of it. Staying on US30 will run you into some of the worst of it, in terms of congestion and sales outlets. PA23, this close to Lancaster, is also busy.

Variation 2: Jersey Surprise Shun (Leg 1) connects with Water Gap Shun (Leg 1) by way of US301—MD213—PA472—PA10 on Maryland's Eastern Shore and in southeastern Pennsylvania.

Eastbound off the Chesapeake Bay Bridge, head north on US301 when it splits with US50. After about five miles turn left onto MD213 and take it all the way to the Pennsylvania line. Immediately after crossing into Pennsylvania turn left onto PA472. Go north on PA10 in Oxford.

This variation performs a fancy weave, leaving Washington and Baltimore to the west, Philadelphia to the east, and Allentown-Bethlehem to the west. MD213 is famous as one of the most beautiful roads in the eastern United States. The feel of the 18th and 19th centuries is still strong in such towns as Centreville, Chestertown and Chesapeake City, and on the old farms and plantations along your route. Here and there an ancient church or burial plot is marked. The road is a meandering two lanes; but if you can feel impatient on this route you are a hopeless turnpiker. Eighteenth-century Chestertown, a river port that had its own tea party of rebellion, is well preserved and deserves a look and a stroll if you can do it. Get a milkshake in the drugstore and amble around the center of town and down to the waterfront. (If you miss your shake here you might try one at the CREE-MEE FREEZE in Cecilton.) Further north, there is a good view from the bridge that takes you over the Chesapeake & Delaware Canal, where ships pass between the Bay and the Delaware River. Crossing US40 and I-95 is not nearly as congested as it appears on the map; a couple of lights and you're on your way.

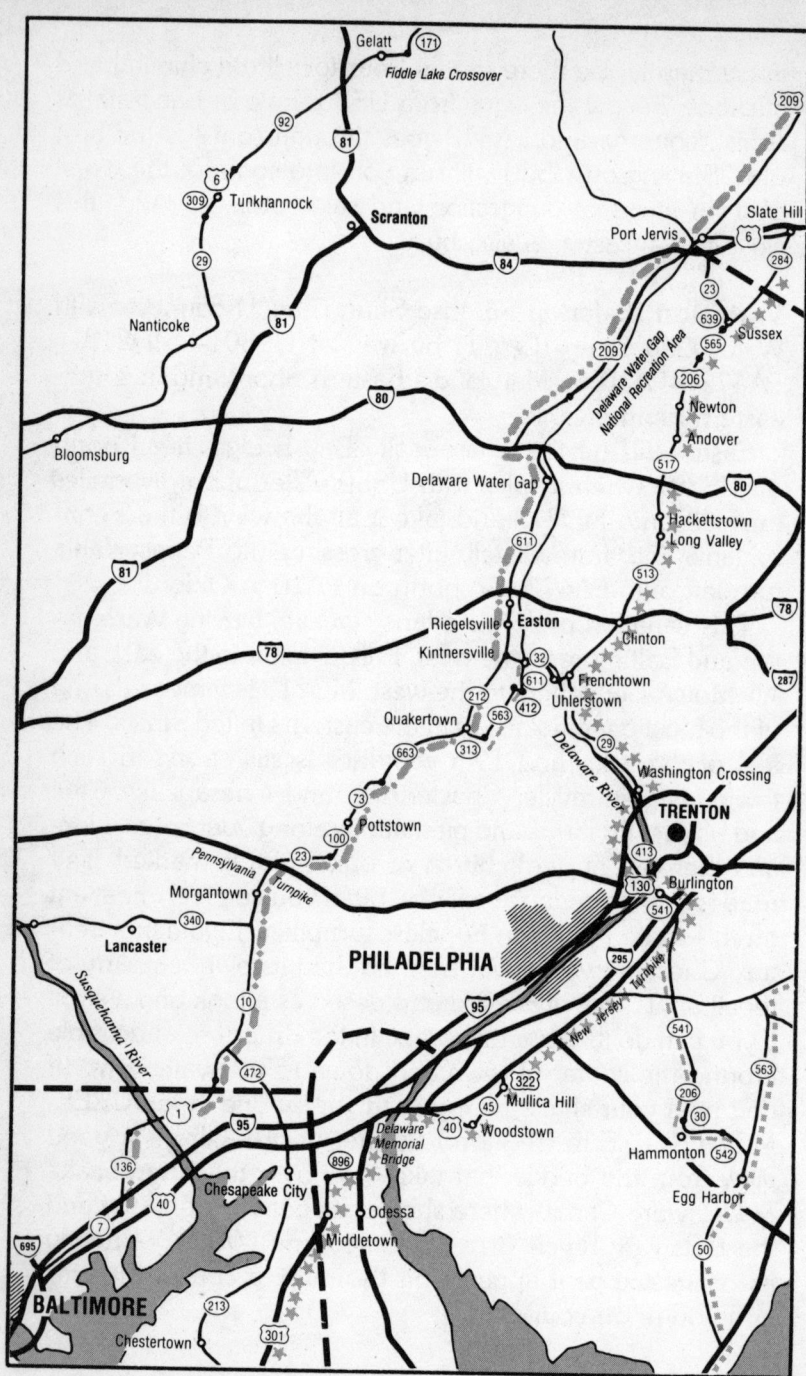

Variations 3 and 4.

Variation 3: Water Gap Shun (Leg 2) connects with Jersey Surprise Shun (Legs 3, 4) southeast of Allentown-Bethlehem, using various routes described below.

• Water Gap Shun *northbound*: At Quakertown follow PA313 instead of PA212. Turn left on PA563, along Nockamixon State Park, then right on PA412 (very briefly) and left on PA611. At Kintnersville on Delaware River turn right on PA32 and then left across river at Uhlerstown. Pick up NJ513 northbound in Frenchtown.

• Water Gap Shun *southbound*: Below Riegelsville, Pennsylvania, continue on PA611 to a left onto PA32. Crossing to New Jersey at Uhlerstown you can pick up NJ29, a right turn, in Frenchtown, which follows Jersey Surprise directions south. You can vary your journey downriver to I-95 (Jersey Surprise Leg 3) by staying on PA32, crossing when and if you want at several bridges along the way.

• Jersey Surprise Shun *northbound*: From NJ29 in Frenchtown turn left, cross over river to PA32 and turn right. Bear right along river when PA32 ends at PA611.

• Jersey Surprise Shun *southbound*: At Frenchtown, New Jersey, cross over river to a right turn on PA32, then go left at PA611. Go right, very briefly, on PA412, and then left past Nockamixon State Park on PA563. Turn right onto PA313 and continue straight on PA663 when PA313 ends on the west side of Quakertown.

For Jersey Surprise northbound and Water Gap southbound, this variation follows the Delaware River from just above Trenton, New Jersey, all the way to Port Jervis, New York, a distance of about 100 miles. You might notice something about the people who live in this area, especially on the Pennsylvania side: they love motorcycles. On warm weekends the husband and wife two-wheeler clubs are out in force on the river roads that are more narrow and certainly more enjoyable to drive than super highways. It's really joy bike riding for grown-ups, some of whom are accountants and grandmothers.

Although Nockamixon State Park has no camping, there is plenty of space by the lake for picnicking. I do not recommend the private campgrounds nearby. They are overpriced and swarming with folks who spend the summer in residence, growing tomatoes in bathtubs beneath strings of patio lights. They are trailer parks pretending to be campgrounds. If you need to camp over, follow the signs from PA563 for Tohickon Campground, but stay at the nice little unsupervised campground across the covered bridge from the Tohickon entrance.

Variation 4: Ferrypike Shun (Leg 3) connects with Jersey Surprise Shun (Leg 3) by way of NJ563—NJ542 (through Batsto—)US30—US206—NJ541, drawing a line, roughly, between Cape May and Trenton, New Jersey.

From Ferrypike Shun and NJ563 go west on NJ542 toward Batsto Village. Just shy of Hammonton turn right onto US30 and then right again after a little more than a mile onto US206 heading north. A few miles beyond the Atsion ranger station of Wharton State Forest bear left onto NJ541. Close one eye to the congestion in Mount Holly and stay on NJ541 through town. You are now on Jersey Surprise Leg 3.

For shunpikers who are traveling a long distance and are not in any particular hurry, this variation creates a route with lots of diversity. From Norfolk north, it includes a bridge-tunnel crossing of the mouth of the Chesapeake Bay, open driving on the Cape Charles/Eastern Shore peninsula, a ferry ride and optional stop in Cape May, the Jersey Pine Barrens and reconstructed Batsto Village, a visit to Washington Crossing and a drive up the Delaware River, lots of New Jersey farm country, a Hudson River crossing and the Taconic highlands, rugged northwestern Connecticut, the Connecticut River and a delightful, heavily forested backcountry approach to Boston. Richmond, Washington, Baltimore, Wilmington, Philadelphia, New York and Hartford are just names on a map; you never even come close to seeing them.

Variation 5: Water Gap Shun (Leg 3) connects with Jersey Surprise Shun (Leg 4, 5) near corner of Pennsylvania, New Jersey and New York, using routes described below.

●Water Gap Shun *northbound*: From Port Jervis, New York, at north end of Delaware Water Gap National Recreation Area, take US6 east to Slate Hill, where you join Leg 4 of Jersey Surprise Shun.

●Water Gap Shun *southbound*: From US209 at Port Jervis, New York, take NY/NJ23 south through High Point State Park. In Sussex follow signs for the airfield—a right turn off NJ23—which puts you on Jersey Surprise Leg 4 heading to Newton, New Jersey.

●Jersey Surprise Shun *northbound*: Heading north past the airfield into Sussex (Leg 4), go left on NJ23 north. After High Point State Park descend into Port Jervis, New York, and pick up US209 northbound.

●Jersey Surprise Shun *southbound*: Stay on US6 west after leaving I-84 (Leg 5 to 4). Go south on US209 in Port Jervis, New York, through Delaware Water Gap National Recreation Area.

High Point State Park and adjoining Stokes State Forest are one of the best-kept outdoor recreation secrets in the East. If you can, camp around the lake at High Point State Park. New Jersey isn't known for its high country, but most of the mountainous terrain it does have is right here. There are lots of wilderness trails, including a portion of the Appalachian Trail. The woods are teeming with birds, especially warblers and red-eyed vireos, and kingfishers frequently swoop down over the lake looking to nail some of its stocked trout. If you have a state fishing license you can join in the fun.

Variation 6: Rivers and Ranges Shun (Leg 4) connects with Water Gap Shun (Leg 3) by way of NY28, between Phoenicia in the Catskills and Kingston on the Hudson River.

This is a beautiful drive along Esopus Creek and Ashokan Reservoir through the heart of the Catskills.

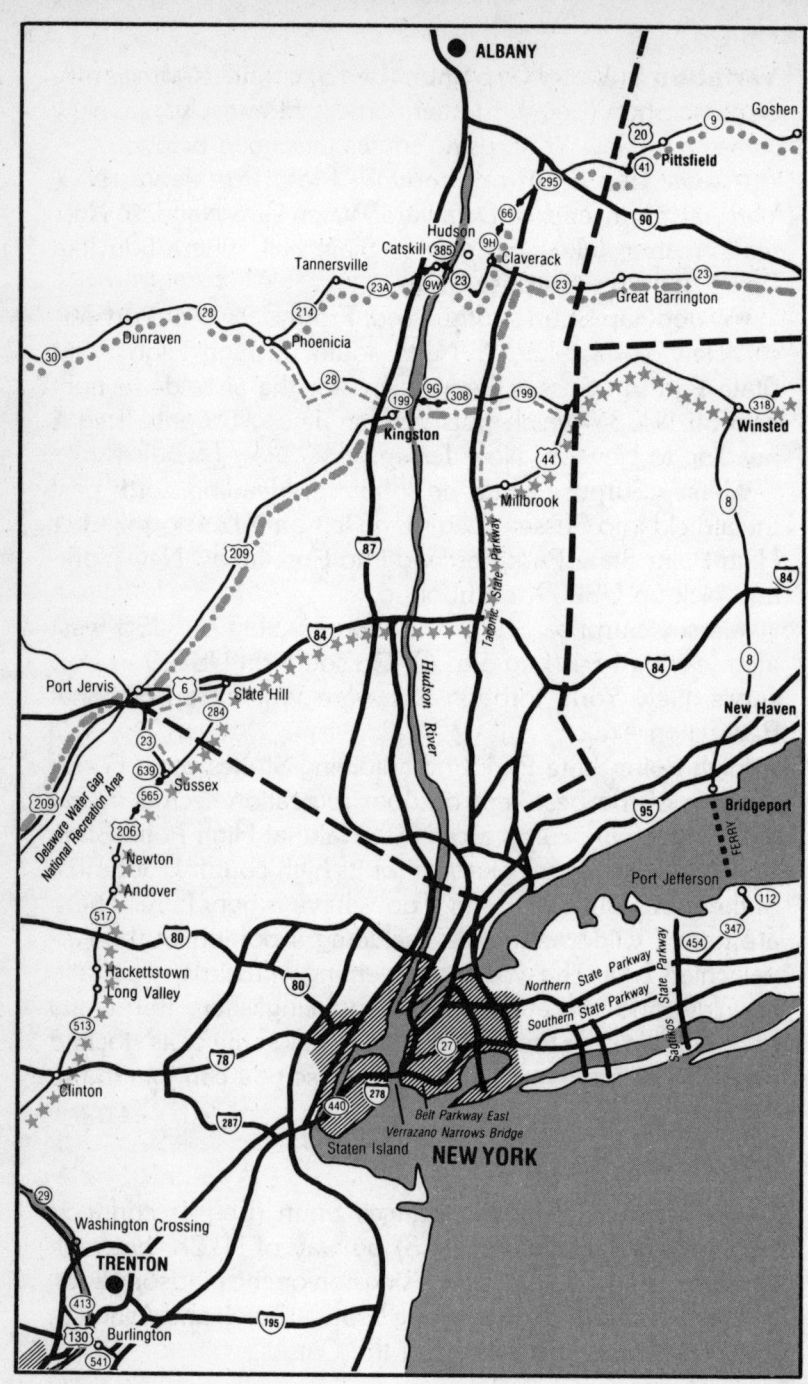

Variations 5 through 10.

(The following variations have a common link—the Taconic Parkway—which parallels the Hudson River.)

Variation 7: Rivers and Ranges Shun (Leg 5) connects with Water Gap Shun (Leg 3) by way of NY/MA23 between Hudson, New York, and Great Barrington, Massachusetts.

East of Hudson stay on NY23 eastbound (a right turn at Claverack). After you cross the Taconic Parkway you are on Water Gap Leg 3.

Variation 8: Water Gap Shun (Leg 3) connects with Rivers and Ranges Shun (Leg 5) by way of NY308—Taconic Parkway—NY295.

East of Kingston, New York, Water Gap Shun picks up Taconic Parkway northbound from NY308. Stay on Parkway almost to its end at I-90, getting off on NY295 near Chatham, New York.

Variation 9: Water Gap Shun (Leg 3) connects with Jersey Surprise Shun (Leg 5) by way of NY308/199—US44 east of Kingston, New York.

Stay on NY308/199 eastbound past Taconic Parkway. Go left when NY199 meets US44 just west of Connecticut state line.

Variation 10: Jersey Surprise Shun (Leg 5) links up with either Water Gap Shun (Leg 3) or Rivers and Ranges Shun (Leg 5) using Taconic Parkway.

From I-84 on Jersey Surprise Shun take Taconic Parkway north. Pick up Water Gap by taking NY23 east from Parkway. Or continue north to NY295 northbound to pick up River and Ranges going to Pittsfield, Massachusetts.

Note for Rivers and Ranges *southbound*: You also have a choice. Instead of continuing south on Leg 5 toward Hudson on NY295, you can get on the Taconic Parkway going south and pick up Water Gap (Leg 3) by taking NY308 west to Kingston, or pick up Jersey Surprise (Leg 5) by taking I-84 west to Middletown, New York.

One last thing. Parkways are roads that prohibit commercial vee-hickles. If you find yourself in heavy traffic in the New Jersey/New York/Connecticut urban areas, try a parkway. There might be a little less traffic, and at least you won't have the Mack Truck bulldog snarling in your rearview mirror. Some of the parkways seem almost rural, especially when trees and bushes are full of leaves to block your view beyond the roadway. Initially you may feel a bit overwhelmed. Locals who drive these roads on a daily basis tend to go very fast, because they have memorized every curve. They like to pretend the evening rush hour is a road rally; first one home wins a martini to settle the nerves. Typical turnpiker behavior. Don't let them intimidate you. It'll drive 'em nuts if you maintain a relaxed shunpiker's pace, and Hula Doll will be proud of you.

Epilogue: One Shunpiker's Beginnings

It was a day like any other on the interstate when Sally Shunshine, who had been born and raised a turnpiker, simply fell off the highway. Her mind was a complete blank when she landed, which was how it was before she fell.

She had no recollection of how it had happened. Of course, she had never remembered anything about driving on the interstates before anyway. Blank was the standard turnpiker state of mind.

Sally found herself sitting upright in her car on a road that turned to the right and vanished into some woods about 200 yards ahead. She'd never seen such a thing. She got out of the car and looked around.

Just then a Model T roadster came out of the woods where the road entered them. As it approached, Sally could see that the driver was a little toad wearing a touring cap, a silk dickey and a tweed jacket. Standing in the rear of the car was a tiny brown-skinned woman all decked out in flowers. She seemed to be dancing. The car passed and the toad waved and called, "It's a lovely day for a drive in the motorcar!" Sally detected an English accent. She waved back and the toad tooted his horn. It sounded like "poop-poop!" The dancing woman smiled and waved, and kept it up until Sally couldn't see her anymore.

There was nobody else on the road after that. The warm, sweet aroma of pine sap and wildflowers tickled Sally's nose, instead of diesel fumes. A chipmunk crossed the road but wasn't in a hurry. He stopped in the middle of the pavement, stood straight up and looked at Sally before continuing on his way. Sally felt the sun on her head, and the light breeze cooled the damp spot on her back that seemed to have melted into the car seat years ago. It was very quiet, but she wasn't scared.

Sally hopped back into the car and headed tentatively toward the bend in the road. As the road turned, she followed it by turning the steering wheel. She'd never had to turn on an interstate, because they always go straight dead ahead. As she entered the woods, her windshield became a rolling display of sunlight and tree shadows. It was frightening at first; the interstates didn't have anything like that, unless you count the huge signs that span the highway and say NEXT EXIT 35 MILES.

Almost as soon as Sally had negotiated the bend to the right, there came a bend to the left. And pretty soon the road curved again, and again. Sally was getting the hang of it and liked the way the car leaned gently into the curves. After a while she noticed the road was following the course of a stream that wound through these woods, and every now and then it crossed over on little bridges and continued along the other bank.

Sally hummed a happy melody that she just made up as she went along. She rolled down the window and stuck her elbow out into the breeze. She waved at a woman driving a tractor in a field, and the woman waved back. When Sally rode over a dip in the road she giggled as her stomach felt the butterflies. At one point she stopped and went wading in the stream. She cupped a handful of cool water and splashed her face and the back of her neck. She plucked a buttercup and held it under her chin as she looked in the rearview mirror; the bright yellow on her skin proved she liked butter.

It had never before occurred to Sally that travel could be fun. She'd always thought travel was a necessary obstacle to being someplace else. At least that's what all the other turnpikers had taught her. But she was having fun now, and she was traveling.

Sally told her turnpiker friends about what she had found on the quiet country roads. Many didn't believe her and roared off angrily into hellbent traffic. That was all right by Sally; she knew her discovery wasn't for everybody. Those who believed, or were curious, pulled off the interstates to see for themselves. It was amazing. After a few turns to the right and turns to the left, they all started feeling pretty good. And they got where they wanted to go too. Along the way some of them stopped at garage sales and antique shops. Some picked fresh blueberries and strawberries right off the plants. Some dropped a fishing line, or visited parks or historic sites. Some paused to hit a bucket of balls at a driving range. They had lunch at local restaurants and diners—not one of them alike—and couldn't believe their ears when the waitress asked, "How would you like that done?"

And because they had shunned the accepted ways of the turnpikes and interstates, this new class of travelers called themselves shunpikers.

Their number is steadily growing.

> *When the people of the world all
>   know beauty as beauty,
> There arises the recognition of
>   ugliness.*
>
>   LAO-TZU

Special thanks to

Deb Amspacher, a troubleshooter whose aim is true;

Ellen McNeirney, who suggested the ferries;

Chris and Barb, who gave me a home base in New England.

More Ways to Enjoy Your Travel on the Eastern Seaboard

Maryland One-Day Trip Book $10.95
America's love affair with trains began in Maryland, and that's one good reason to explore the Land of Pleasant Living. There are 189 other good reasons presented county by county in this, Jane Ockershausen Smith's sixth One-Day Trip Book. Come see the fabulous National Aquarium, art collections, rugged Appalachian scenery, a museum of huge cannon, horse farms, vineyards and much more. A topical cross reference, calendar of events and index are included.

Adventure Vacations in Five Mid-Atlantic States $9.95
Adventure takes on a new, expanded meaning in this comprehensive guide to challenging vacations in NC, WV, VA, MD and PA. Hiking, biking, trail riding, canoeing and rafting are some choices; digging for artifacts and mystery clues, learning to dance, weave, paint, fish and elderhosteling are a few others. Each entry offers tips on planning, costs, equipment and special attractions.

The Walker Washington Guide $6.95
The sixth edition of the "guide's guide to Washington," completely revised by Katharine Walker, builds on a 25-year reputation as the top general guide to the nation's capital. Its 320 pages are packed with museums, galleries, hotels, restaurants, theaters, shops, churches, as well as sights. Beautiful maps and photos. Indispensable.

Unique Meeting Places in Greater Washington $11.95
Tired of parties in the same old hotel banquet rooms? Why not hold your next event at a President's home, embassy mansion, art gallery, museum, plantation, aquarium or aboard a ship? This one-of-a-kind guide describes nearly 100 unusual, distinctive meeting and party sites in the Capital area. Capacities, rates, catering arrangements and other planning information provided.

Florida One-Day Trip Book $5.95
After you've done Disney, discover the real Florida. This breezy guide by *Orlando Sentinel* columnist Ed Hayes features 52 offbeat excursions in the Sunshine State's central region, from America's oldest city and sub-tropical gardens to Spook Hill, Fort Christmas, a serpentarium and the Spongeorama at historic Tarpon Springs.

Call It Delmarvalous $7.95
To properly appreciate the Delmarva (Delaware, Maryland, Virginia) Peninsula, it's best to know how to talk, cook and "feel to hum" there, preferably at the local far hall (where farmen gather to foit fars). This delightful introduction shows you what being a "peninchula" native is all about, including recipes and a Delmarva dictionary.

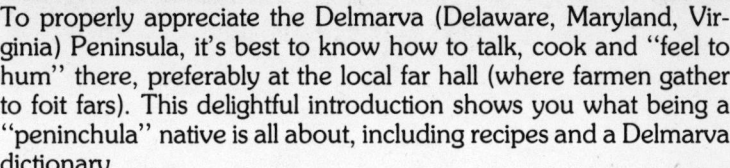

Virginia One-Day Trip Book $8.95
From the Shenandoah Valley and Blue Ridge peaks, across the piedmont and down ancient rivers spilling into bountiful Chesapeake Bay, Virginia is unmatched in beauty, history and variety. Divided into seven geographic regions, these 101 day-trip delights make this the perfect guide for anyone who is anywhere in the Old Dominion.

Philadelphia One-Day Trip Book $8.95
And you thought Independence Hall and the Lbierty Bell were all Philadelphia had to offer? Don't overlook Norman Rockwell Museum, Pottsgrove Mansion, Daniel Boone Homestead, Covered Bridges, Amish Farms and scores of other exciting excursions.

ORDER BLANK. Mail with check to:

EPM Publications, Box 490, McLean, VA 22101

Title	Qty	Price	Amount
A Shunpiker's Guide to the Northeast			
		Subtotal	
	Virginia residents add 4½% tax		
	Add $2 shpg. first book, $1 ea. add'l.		
		Total	

Name _____

Street _____

City _____ State _____ Zip _____

Remember to enclose names, addresses and enclosure cards for gift purchases. Prices are subject to change. Write or call for free catalog: 703-442-7810.